Top Business Psychology Models

50 transforming ideas for leaders, consultants and coaches

Stefan Cantore and
Jonathan Passmore

KoganPage

LONDON PHILADELPHIA NEW DELHI

This book is dedicated to Florence & Jóhannes

First published in Great Britain and the United States in 2012 by Kogan Page Limited

120 Pentonville Road	1518 Walnut Street, Suite 1100	4737/23 Ansari Road
London N1 9JN	Philadelphia PA 19102	Daryaganj
United Kingdom	USA	New Delhi 110002
www.koganpage.com		India

© Stefan Cantore and Jonathan Passmore, 2012

ISBN   978 0 7494 6465 3
E-ISBN   978 0 7494 6466 0

British Library Cataloguing-in-Publication Data

A CIP record for this book is available from the British Library.

Library of Congress Cataloging-in-Publication Data

Passmore, Jonathan.
  Top business psychology models : 50 transforming ideas for leaders, consultants, and coaches / Jonathan Passmore, Stefan Cantore.
    p. cm.
  ISBN 978-0-7494-6465-3 – ISBN 978-0-7494-6466-0   1. Psychology, Industrial.
2. Organizational change–Management.   3. Interpersonal relations.
4. Teams in the workplace.   I. Cantore, Stefan.   II. Title.
  HF5548.8.P28 2012
  658.4'092019–dc23

                                                                              2012007725

Typeset by Graphicraft Ltd, Hong Kong
Printed and bound in India by Replika Press Pvt Ltd

CONTENTS

ACKNOWLEDGEMENTS

The authors wish to thank a number of people for their invaluable contributions. Bridget Grenville-Cleave for her help with the concept of the book and selecting useful models for inclusion. Celia Payne, Mark Palin and other colleagues who have provided thoughtful feedback on early drafts. Martina at Kogan Page for her encouragement and challenge. Katharine, Geoff Kent and our families, friends and colleagues who have stuck with us through the writing process. Thanks go particularly to the many researchers, academics, practitioners and authors whose ideas we have incorporated into this book. It is their hard work that has formed the basis for ours and it is to them that we are indebted.

ABOUT THE AUTHORS

Stefan Cantore

Stefan is Senior Teaching Fellow in Organizational Behaviour and Human Resource Management at the School of Management, University of Southampton, UK. He also maintains a leadership and organizational development consulting practice. His passion is to help leaders and organizations use conversation as a process for change. He is a qualified coach and has Master's degrees in both People and Organizational Development and Business Administration. He is currently researching the nature and practice of 'Conversational Consulting' as a Doctoral candidate at Middlesex University.

Stefan's career includes spells as CEO of an NHS Hospital and Community Services organization and as Director of a System Transformation team working across health, social care and the voluntary sectors. He co-authored *Appreciative Inquiry for Change Management* with Jonathan and Sarah Lewis. Stefan can be contacted at **stefancantore2@tiscali.co.uk**.

Dr Jonathan Passmore

Jonathan is a business psychologist in a private practice. He is also a professor of Leadership and Coaching. He has five degrees and has an international reputation for his work in coaching, change and leadership. He has published 14 books on the themes of leadership, personal development and change, including editing the *Association for Coaching* series of coaching titles for Kogan Page. He consults and speaks at conferences across the world from the United States to Europe and Asia. He has published over 30 peer-related papers in a wide variety of journals and over 50 papers in magazines and trade journals. He was awarded the AC Global Coaching Award for his contribution to practice and research in 2010. Jonathan can be contacted at **jonathancpassmore@yahoo.co.uk**.

FOREWORD

There is nothing more practical than a good theory. What a magnificent insight Kurt Lewin had over 50 years ago. It was valuable and useful insight then and – it's still valid today. And, I would add, more than ever. We live in an ever complex, global and diverse organizational world where to remain competitive, organizations need to use and apply tools (eg, models) that help them understand their human capital (ie, how they think, feel and what they do). That is the motivation behind this volume – to provide leaders, HR executives, managers and coaches with a practical translation of the most impactful theories and models of human behaviour published in organizational science. And to that, I say, bravo Stefan and Jonathan!

This is exactly what our science needs – more translations. We need more translations of what we know about human behaviour at work and more translations of our wonderful theories and models. Our theories and models are the foundation of what we do – they are our guide. They provide the blueprint for our empirical work. They help us make sense of our findings. And, more importantly, provide the framework for practice. Stefan and Jonathan have taken 50 of our theories (and models) and have translated their underpinnings and eloquently illustrated how each guides practice – how each tells us something about what people think, feel and do in organizations (and beyond, I'll add). They cover notable theories like Maslow, Myers-Briggs, and goal setting theory, attribution theory and more. But they also cover how tools and methods (eg, rating scales) can be used to assess and diagnose relative human behaviour. There is, indeed, a chapter (or more) for every leader of an organization.

This volume provides a great service to those in practices, and to those in organizational science. Certainly, it made me reflect and reaffirmed that there is nothing more practical than a good theory. We need more books of this kind. We need more translations of our science. Stefan and Jonathan have paved the way – thank you!! Thank you for this one-of-a-kind gem.

Eduardo Salas, Ph.D.
Pegasus & University Trustee Chair Professor
Department of Psychology
Institute for Simulation & Training
University of Central Florida
Orlando, Fl

Introduction

Thirty minutes is all you have on a train journey to prepare a snappy, intelligent and evidenced-based presentation to a management team on improving performance. We have all been there! You don't want to confuse them with jargon nor do you want to sound like you are making it up as you go along. What you need are a couple of inspirational tested ideas to add a bit of weight to what you plan to say. This book has been written with you in mind.

Maybe you're a leader responding to the challenges of a competitive business environment. Or you are a manager on your way up. Difficult relationships seem to make the going even tougher. Changes are harder to make with so many stakeholders to take into account. You wonder if anyone has been there before and has any useful wisdom you can borrow. This book is for you.

Perhaps you are a coach or group facilitator with an interest in psychology and its practical application in business and organizational contexts. You've probably picked up some of the ideas and buzzwords along the way but want to know about the science to support the ideas you have come across. You want to get it right from a trusted source, not pick up the misrepresented ideas from some internet blog. A quick browse through these 50 chapters will help you think about your own development and equip you to authoritatively share ideas with clients and coachees.

You are responsible for leading a change project. You find people are stuck and not able, or willing, to move forward. Perhaps you also feel stuck as you try to help them! Use this book to open up new ideas and facilitate creative ways forward.

If you are a student of business psychology with assignments and projects to complete and want a resource that is clear, succinct and well referenced, this is a book for you too.

Business psychology is a catch-all phrase. In this book we define it as 'studies and theories which help us to understand or explain human behaviour, emotions and cognition at work'. Flick through the contents pages of any sizeable textbook on the subject and you will see what we mean. Plenty of material tends to be drawn from the early part of the 20th century. Much also comes from more recent work by organizational, behavioural and social psychologists. More recently, new knowledge is being sourced from positive, educational neuropsychology.

But it doesn't stop there. Researchers look increasingly at the overlaps between domains of knowledge to spot the interconnections. Links between human physiology, spirituality, philosophy and psychology are all fertile ground for new theories. As a result, there are fuzzy boundaries between aspects of business psychology and many of these other areas of practice which have implications for our performance at work.

Our rationale is to pick business and positive psychology ideas that:

- have been tried and tested by us and our colleagues over many years; they work well with a wide range of clients and organizations in many contexts;

- are practical and usually have some sort of evidence base to support them;

- you can quickly get to grips with and not short-change either the idea or your audience;

- come from the many different domains of business and positive psychology, which adds variety and hopefully will spark you into digging around in the literature;

- are a mix of well-recognized 'classics' and ideas whose time, we think, is just about to come;

- encourage a positive, optimistic and appreciative outlook on life and the work we are all engaged in.

We've written short chapters, around 1,000 words, knowing that time is precious and that you want something that is to the point. We have tried to go back to source books/papers to enhance accuracy. We have also offered detailed references to support the material, including pointers for further reading if you wish to follow up this short summary with more detail. However, in doing so we appreciate that there is a risk we will fail to capture some of the subtle details of some of the studies, or fully reflect the counter-arguments or wider research. We have tried our best to be as accurate as possible, but ultimately any mistake is ours.

To help place each model or framework we have tried to categorize each under one of three headings: Individuals, Groups and Organizations. Some frameworks, of course, fall into more than one heading and we have tried to select the one we felt it fitted best.

Each chapter is split into four short sections. In the first part we aim to set out the 'Big idea'. This aims to explain in around 500 words what the framework or theory is all about. In the second section we explain the implications of the theory, what it might mean for those working in an organization. In the third section we offer some of the limitations and counterarguments. Fourth, we offer a leadership challenge. Many of the theories are great at explaining the words, but we wanted to bring these alive and contribute to your leadership development. The leadership challenge encourages you to play with or try out some of the ideas from the chapter. Finally, we offer a selection of key references, including one or two references for further reading, if you want to explore the ideas in more depth.

Researching and writing this book have been an absorbing and enlightening process. We hope you experience something similar as you read and use it.

You can find out more details about the ideas in the book and some additional material on our website Mondays Psychologists – **www.mondayspsychologists.co.uk**.

PART ONE
The individual at work

Introduction
What makes individuals tick?

Personalities

Leaders are continually looking to better understand their people in the search for improving performance. This first part of the book captures a wide range of psychological theories, supported by some evidence about how individuals think and behave in a work context. The focus is on differences between individuals, their personalities and the way they interact with their colleagues, managers and the environment. We also look at ways in which people can get a better understanding of their own preferences and approach to work. It's this self-awareness that not only helps employees cope with challenges but is vital for leaders if they are to manage their own reactions and role-model positive behaviour.

Change

The impact of change on individuals in a work context varies hugely. We take a look at some of the more recent theories about how leaders can tailor their mindsets and actions to create positive, energy-filled responses to change while acknowledging the loss and emotional transitions that people experience. This part of the book also considers how leaders can effectively support people through change even when they are manifesting wildly different reactions.

Decisions

Given that one of the most critical decisions a leader will take is whom to employ, or whom to fire, the theories we have chosen offer insights into matching people with roles. There are plenty of psychological tests on the market claiming to help leaders make decisions about whom to employ or promote. We offer ideas that help you evaluate their claims.

Putting someone into a job is just the start. To get the best out of them you need to commit to develop them. We have included models that will help leaders do that practically. These ideas will shape attitudes and behaviours that ultimately deliver results and achieve business goals.

Your leadership

Whatever your role, our belief is that if you are reading this book you are probably contributing in some way to the leadership of one or more organizations. The ideas in this part of the book are in here because we think they also offer you a personal challenge about how you express that leadership and what you can do to develop it.

What makes people do things?

Maslow's hierarchy of needs

The big idea

Abraham Maslow (1908–70) is one of the most well known psychologists of the 20th century, and his theory of human motivation, first published in a paper towards the end of the Second World War (Maslow, 1943), remains one of the most popular theories explaining human behaviour.

In a nutshell, Maslow argued that people have a variety of needs and that their behaviour at work, or elsewhere, is directed towards getting these needs met. His initial model set out five classes of human need:

1 Physiological: to have the food, drink and sex you require. He described these as the most basic and biological needs.

2 Safety: to be in an environment that is safe physically and psychologically.

3 Social: to have a sense of relationship with people as individuals and groups.

4 Esteem: to believe yourself to be successful and worthwhile in your own eyes and the eyes of others.

5 Self-actualization: to desire to become all that you are capable of becoming.

Maslow (1954) proposed that the needs are activated in a hierarchical manner. So once basic physiological needs are satisfied, people will aim to meet their safety needs and so on up the list. He defined the first three needs on the list as 'deficiency needs' which, if not met, will prevent the person from becoming a healthy person. The top two, esteem and self-actualization (a term he coined and which has now become part of everyday language), are 'growth needs' which help people develop their full potential as humans.

FIGURE 1.1   Maslow's hierarchy of needs

Need	Motivation to satisfy need
Need for self-actualization	Challenging projects, opportunities for innovation and creativity, learning at a high level
Need for self-esteem	Important projects, recognition of strength, intelligence, prestige and status
Social needs – belonging	Acceptance, group membership, association with successful team, love and affection
Need for safety and security	Physical safety, economic security, freedom from threats, comfort, peace
Physical survival needs	Water, food, sleep, warmth, health, exercise, sex

Maslow suggested that the hierarchy is open-ended, so once we reach the top we become aware of even more potential in us to grow than we at first appreciated. This spurs us on to seek more opportunities to develop. In later work Maslow (Maslow, Frager and Fadiman, 1970) expanded the notion of self-actualization to include personal growth needs, the appreciation of beauty, and self-transcendance (to find something beyond oneself and to commit to helping others grow).

The theory has frequently been applied to understanding behaviour in the workplace. Figure 1.1 illustrates some of the ways in which this has been done.

So what?

While Maslow never offered specific applications in his writings, management theorists have subsequently readily suggested what managers can do to motivate employees. These recommendations range from ensuring safe work environments to pension schemes, positive team working, job titles, promotion opportunities, public recognition awards and development opportunities. These all make sense to most people and have meant that Maslow's ideas have remained popular. It is, in part, the all-encompassing nature of the theory that has contributed to its longevity.

What remains problematic is being able to be clear both about what needs people are trying to meet at work at any point in time, and what actions managers can reasonably take to meet those needs in a way that motivates for better performance. This has consistently been viewed as a major flaw in the theory. Critics like Buchanan and Huczynski (1997) say that what works for one person may not work for another. People try to meet a range of needs at the same time and not necessarily in a systematic hierarchical order.

These critiques have been confirmed by researchers over the years (for example, Neher, 1991; Salancik and Pfeffer, 1977; Ventegodt, Merrick and Andersen, 2003; Wahba and Bridwell, 1976). The consensus is that no empirical research has confirmed the validity of the theory in its entirety. Buchanan and Huczynski (1997: 62) helpfully describe Maslow's theory as more like a social philosophy than a 'psychological theory', with its concerns about the values implicit in the idea of the 'good life'. Hofstede (1980) added to the criticism by arguing that it was middle-class American ideals that Maslow wrote about, rather than a more universal approach to motivation which needs to incorporate a multicultural perspective.

To be fair to Maslow, he acknowledged at the outset that the hierarchy model was not a perfect one. He wrote of reversal in the order of the hierarchy being observed at times and that all individuals may not require all needs to be met under certain circumstances. He also recognized that there may be determinants of behaviour other than specific motivations.

What else?

In spite of the criticism, Maslow's model has remained popular for reasons that include:

- the way it acknowledges that human beings have needs that they strive to meet;
- the prompt it has given managers to think about what they are doing to motivate their staff;
- its positive view of human nature and the recognition of the seemingly innate sense in people to strive to improve;
- the use other theorists and researchers like Alderfer (1972) have made of Maslow's thinking to refine and develop our understanding of human motivation;
- the acknowledgement it gives to the notion that human behaviour is influenced by a number of very different motives.

Abraham Maslow's theory underpins the thinking behind what he called the new discipline of humanistic psychology which came to the fore in the 1950s. This school of psychology holds the view that human beings are essentially good and that the role of psychology is to investigate what will help them reach their full potential. In recent years, Maslow has also been credited with being one of the founding fathers of the positive psychology movement (Seligman and Csíkszentmihályi, 2000).

Leadership challenge

What parts of your life motivate you to be all you can be (self-actualization)? How can you bring these feelings into the way you motivate your team?

More help

Key references

Maslow, A H (1954) *Motivation and Personality*, New York: Harper & Brothers
Maslow, A H (1943) A theory of human motivation, *Psychological Review*, **50** (4), p 370
Maslow, A H, Frager, R and Fadiman, J (1970) *Motivation and Personality*, New York: Harper and Row
Alderfer, C P (1972) *Existence, Relatedness, and Growth: Human needs in organizational settings*, New York: Free Press

Other references

Buchanan, D A and Huczynski, A (1997) *Organizational Behaviour: An introductory text*, Prentice Hall, Harlow
Hofstede, G (1980) Motivation, leadership, and organization: do American theories apply abroad? *Organizational Dynamics*, **9** (1), pp 42–63
Neher, A (1991) Maslow's theory of motivation, *Journal of Humanistic Psychology*, **31** (3), p 89
Salancik, G R and Pfeffer, J (1977) An examination of need-satisfaction models of job attitudes, *Administrative Science Quarterly*, **22**, pp 427–56
Seligman, M E P and Csíkszentmihályi, M (2000) Positive psychology: an introduction, *American Psychologist*, **55** (1), p 5
Ventegodt, S, Merrick, J and Andersen, N J (2003) Quality of life theory III. Maslow revisited, *Scientific World Journal*, **3**, pp 1050–7
Wahba, M A and Bridwell, L G (1976) Maslow reconsidered: a review of research on the need hierarchy theory, *Organizational Behavior and Human Performance*, **15** (2), pp 212–40

How can we become more engaged with work?
Flow

The big idea

The concept of flow, or optimal experience, is cited extensively in positive psychology literature. It was first investigated and described by US psychology professor Mihály Csíkszentmihályi in the 1960s and 1970s. Flow is a 'holistic experience that people feel when they act with total involvement' (Csíkszentmihályi, 1975). Perhaps a more descriptive definition is 'the state in which people are so involved in an activity that nothing else seems to matter; the experience itself is so enjoyable that people will do it even at great cost, for the sheer sake of doing it' (Csíkszentmihályi, 1991).

Csíkszentmihályi's interest in the nature of all-consuming experiences first began while observing painters and musicians getting totally immersed in their art. They often seemed oblivious to the outside world and totally focused on their creative process. He researched how that happens psychologically and what can be done to encourage it in a range of work and leisure contexts.

Using a research technique called the experience sampling method (ESM), he kept track of people's experiences by prompting them, via a pager activated at random times, to write down in a log what they were thinking and feeling. Analysis showed that flow happened when people were doing those things in which they were most interested. Subsequently, Csíkszentmihályi refined his ideas and suggests that flow is likely to happen when a number of components are present:

1 Clear goals that, while challenging, are still attainable.
2 Immediate feedback.
3 Knowing that the task is doable; a balance between personal skill level and the challenge presented.
4 Strong concentration and focused attention.
5 The activity is intrinsically rewarding.

6   Feelings of serenity; a loss of feelings of self-consciousness.

7   Timelessness; a distorted sense of time; feeling so focused on the present that time seems to pass very quickly.

8   Feelings of personal control over the situation and the outcome.

9   Lack of awareness of physical needs.

10   Complete focus on the activity itself.

(Adapted from Csíkszentmihályi, 1997)

Of these ten components, much of the literature indicates that for flow to be experienced the first three are probably the most significant. Csíkszentmihályi also suggests that certain types of people are more likely to experience flow than others. He uses the term 'autotelic personality' to describe people who are highly intrinsically motivated. They are less concerned about rewards such as pay or publicity, but much more focused on gaining satisfaction through their own curiosity and determination (Csíkszentmihályi, 1997). There is not yet clear evidence that such types of people do actually experience flow more than others.

When a person does experience flow they may feel completely absorbed, sense themselves outside reality, serene and extremely happy. They are likely to be focused and highly productive, with an inner clarity about what needs to be accomplished.

So what?

If managers can combine challenge, skill and some of the other components, the potential for flow to benefit business is obvious. It may be that developing a workforce with a high level of flow state will lead to high performance. Csíkszentmihályi suggests that managers can create environments for work groups in which flow is more likely to occur by:

- providing spaces where wall charts, pictures and the availability of creative materials promote engagement and moving around by team members;
- clarifying the goals and when they need to be achieved, taking care to explain how doing so will enhance the performance of the company;
- encouraging the development of existing groups rather than starting from scratch with a new one;
- stimulating play and fun;
- welcoming differences between people as an opportunity to enhance creativity.

(Adapted from Csíkszentmihályi, 2004)

Flow prompts feelings of enjoyment and satisfaction when a job is done well. Enhanced performance in work contexts as a result of flow has been reported over the years. Facing challenges that are slightly beyond a person's level of comfort also prompts skill development and personal growth. One flow experience can lead on to the desire for more and so create a virtuous cycle of performance enhancement.

People experience flow when working hard to finish a job, playing games or absorbed on the internet. These are contexts in which they have control, understand the rules and have clear, desirable outcomes. By implication, anything managers can do to make work routines feel like 'games' is likely to increase the chances of flow experiences (Nielsen and Cleal, 2010).

What else?

Flow is quite a broad concept so the language to describe it can vary from culture to culture. While Csíkszentmihályi has popularized the ideas in Western psychology, very similar ideas can be found in world religions such as Buddhism, Taoism and Islam. Capturing data about flow is almost always done using the ESM. External verification by observing flow behaviour is not possible given this self-report method (Larson and Csíkszentmihályi, 1983). There is scope for strengthening the evidence base for flow by combining self-reports, observations and neurological measurements.

Leadership challenge

Recall a time when you have been fully absorbed in your work. What made that happen? What lessons can you take from this experience into your team?

More help

Key references

Csíkszentmihályi, M (1991) *Flow: The psychology of optimal experience: Steps toward enhancing the quality of life*, Harper Collins, New York
Csíkszentmihályi, M (2004) *Good Business: Leadership, flow, and the making of meaning*, Penguin, New York

Other references

Csíkszentmihályi, M (1997) *Finding Flow: The psychology of engagement with everyday life*, Basic Books, New York
Csíkszentmihályi, M (1975) *Beyond Boredom and Anxiety: The experience of play in work and games*, Jossey-Bass, San Francisco
Larson, R and Csíkszentmihályi, M (1983) The experience sampling method, *New Directions for Methodology of Social and Behavioral Science*, 15, pp 41–56
Nielsen, K and Cleal, B (2010) Predicting flow at work: investigating the activities and job characteristics that predict flow states at work, *Journal of Occupational Health Psychology*, 15 (2), pp 180–90

How can people develop their self-awareness?

Mindfulness

The big idea

Mindfulness is a state of focused, non-judgemental attention on the present. Mindfulness originated as a spiritual practice in Buddhist teaching, but in recent years has been adopted by Western psychology. As mindfulness has moved from East to West, and into the workplace, the religious element has been removed and the practice adapted for a wide range of purposes.

Professor Jon Kabat-Zinn is recognized as the leading thinker and practitioner in the field, having established the Center for Mindfulness in Medicine, Health Care, and Society at the University of Massachusetts Medical School in the early 1980s. His work is focused primarily on the development of mindfulness practice as an integral aspect of treatment for stress, depression, pain and a range of other conditions. Kabat-Zinn defines mindfulness at its most basic as 'paying attention on purpose moment by moment without judging' (Kabat-Zinn *et al*, 1992). Hefferon and Boniwell (2011) have pointed out that it is not about deliberately changing your thinking, nor is it to be confused with positive thinking. Mindfulness involves watching thought itself.

A more technical definition is offered by the psychologist Ellen Langer. She describes mindfulness as:

> a state of active awareness characterized by the continual creation and refinement of categories, an openness to new information, and a willingness to view contexts from multiple perspectives.
>
> (Langer, 1989)

Langer suggests that attention is also given to the other side of the coin, which she labels 'mindlessness', the routine set of processes that people follow in their lives without thinking (Langer, 2000).

Given the different perspectives on the topic, it can be confusing to understand how to put mindfulness into practice. We suggest a series of steps. The first step involves the self-regulation of attention so that it is maintained on immediate experience, thereby allowing for increased recognition of mental events in the present moment. The second step involves adopting a particular orientation towards one's experiences in the present moment, an orientation that is characterized by curiosity, openness and acceptance (Bishop *et al*, 2004).

So what?

Mindfulness can be applied to a wide range of situations and has value for those in organizations and leading others, as well as for coaches and trainers. In a work context, mindfulness is said to offer a wide range of benefits for employees and organizations, which is being increasingly taken up by organizations seeking performance improvement.

At an individual level, research findings suggest that meditation, including mindfulness, can contribute to physiological, psychological and transpersonal well-being and it may help identify and actualize human strengths (Shapiro, Schwartz and Santerre, 2005). For example, at a physiological level mindfulness has been shown to positively impact a large variety of factors such as blood pressure (McCraty, 2003) and the immune system (Rein and McCraty, 1995). Perhaps more relevant to the workplace are the numerous aspects of the psychology impact of mindfulness, including: job strain (Cropley and Purvis, 2003), job satisfaction and vision (Kriger and Hanson, 1999), self-compassion (Neff, Hsieh and Dejitterat, 2005; Shapiro *et al*, 2005), emotional awareness and interpersonal sensitivity (Shefy and Sadler-Smith, 2006) and learning (Yeganeh, 2006). These factors can in turn contribute to improving health and well-being in the workplace, thus reducing absenteeism and occupational health costs, and foster more effective skills in managing conflict, stress, personnel, communication and leadership.

Mindfulness has been shown to positively impact several areas that are directly responsible for business performance, among them: safety culture (Hopkins, 2002), conflict resolution (Riskin, 2004), creativity (Langer and Piper, 1987) and decision making (Fiol and O'Connor, 2003).

Given these results, Karl Weick has argued that it is possible for organizations that commit to mindfulness practices to build collective mindfulness which offers benefits in terms of safer ways of working and better outcomes (Weick and Sutcliffe, 2001). While marginal for some organizations, safe practices can be critical in high-risk and safety-critical environments such as oil and gas exploration, the nuclear industry and transportation.

What else?

So what can the modern leader do to achieve these gains? The first step is to understand mindfulness practice: what it is and what it involves. A training course in mindfulness will offer insights into what and how.

At a more practical level, Passmore and Marianetti have offered some steps which most trainers, coaches and leaders could use every day as part of their route to improving concentration, focus and energy. These include undertaking short three- or four-minute mindfulness meditations or body scans at the start of the day or lunch break, being aware of the wandering mind during meetings and conversations and seeking to bring the focus back to the here and now of the meeting or the conversation (Passmore and Marianetti, 2007).

Leadership challenge

Find a quiet space and then stop everything you are doing. Close your eyes and focus on your breathing. For the next two minutes be aware of your breathing, and if your mind wanders to think about other things, bring it back to focus on your breathing. At the end of the first two minutes, start to move your focus to an awareness of the different parts of your body. Start with your head and work down through your neck, shoulders, back, chest, until you reach your toes. Be aware of any sensations in the different muscles of your body, any tightness or your body touching a chair or the floor. Aim to spend two minutes scanning your body from head to toe. Finally, spend one minute back focusing on your breath, and targeting your breath towards any places of tightness or discomfort. Imagine them feeling lighter and more relaxed.

More help

Key reference

Kabat-Zinn, J (1990) *Full catastrophe living: Using the wisdom of your body and mind to face stress, pain, and illness*, Delta, Brooklyn, NY

Other references

Bishop, S R, Lau, M, Shapiro, S *et al* (2004) Mindfulness: A proposed operational definition, *Clinical Psychology: Science and Practice*, **11** (3), pp 230–41
Cropley, M and Purvis, L J (2003) Job strain and rumination about work issues during leisure time: a diary study, *European Journal of Work and Organizational Psychology*, **12**, pp 195–207

Fiol, C M and O'Connor, E J (2003) Waking up! Mindfulness in the face of bandwagons, *Academy of Management Review*, 28, pp 54–70

Hefferon, K and Boniwell, I (2011) *Positive Psychology: Theory, research and applications*, Open University Press, Milton Keynes

Hopkins, A (2002) *Safety Culture, Mindfulness and Safe Behaviour: Converging ideas?* Working Paper, National Research Centre for Occupational Health and Safety Regulation, Australia

Kabat-Zinn, J, Massion, A O, Kristeller, J *et al* (1992) Effectiveness of a meditation-based stress reduction program in the treatment of anxiety disorders, *American Journal of Psychiatry*, 149 (7), pp 936–43

Kriger, M P and Hanson, B J (1999) A value-based paradigm for creating truly healthy organizations, *Journal of Organizational Change Management*, 12 (4), pp 302–17

Langer, E J (1989) Minding matters: the consequences of mindlessness–mindfulness, *Advances in Experimental Social Psychology*, 22, pp 137–73

Langer, E J (2000) Mindful learning, *Current Directions in Psychological Science*, 9 (6), pp 220–3

Langer, E J and Piper, A (1987) The prevention of mindlessness, *Journal of Personality and Social Psychology*, 53, pp 280–7

McCraty, R M (2003) Impact of a workplace stress reduction program on blood pressure and emotional health in hypertensive employees, *Journal of Alternative and Complementary Medicine*, 9 (3), pp 355–69

Neff, K D, Hsieh, Y P and Dejitterat, K (2005) Self-compassion, achievement goals, and coping with academic failure, *Self and Identity*, 4, pp 263–87

Passmore, J and Marianetti, O (2007) The role of mindfulness in coaching, *The Coaching Psychologist*, 3 (3), pp 131–8

Rein, G and McCraty, R M (1995) Effects of positive and negative emotions on salivary IgA, *Journal for the Advancement of Medicine*, 8 (2), pp 87–105

Riskin, L L (2004) Mindfulness: foundational training for dispute resolution, *Journal of Legal Education*, 54 (1), pp 79–90

Shapiro, S L, Schwartz, G E and Santerre, C (2005) Meditation and positive psychology, in *Handbook of Positive Psychology*, ed C R Snyder and S J Lopez, pp 632–45, Oxford University Press, New York

Shefy, E, and Sadler-Smith, E (2006) Applying holistic principles in management development, *Journal of Management Development*, 25 (4), pp 368–85

Weick, K E and Sutcliffe, K M (2001) *Managing the Unexpected: Assuring high performance in an age of complexity*, Jossey-Bass, San Francisco

Yeganeh, B (2006) *Mindful Experiential Learning*, PhD thesis, Case Western Reserve University, Department of Organizational Behavior

04

Helping others to set goals
The GROW model

The big idea

GROW is a four-stage coaching model developed by Graham Alexander and Sir John Whitmore in the 1980s, when both were working in consulting. The model can be used to structure a one-to-one coaching or mentoring conversation. Coaches work through the four stages: to help their coachee identify the *Goals*, review their *Reality*, generate *Options* and develop a *Way forward* or *Will* (Figure 4.1).

In the goal phase the coach helps the coachee to identify an objective that they want to work towards. The coach uses open questions and summaries to help the coachee to clarify and refine the goal towards a more specific and measurable objective (a SMART goal).

FIGURE 4.1   The GROW model

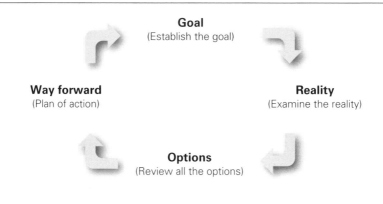

Goal
(Establish the goal)

Way forward
(Plan of action)

Reality
(Examine the reality)

Options
(Review all the options)

In the second phase of the work the coach encourages the coachee to reflect on their current performance and to draw on evidence. This evidence may include 360° feedback data, appraisal information or general feedback. It is also likely to include the coachee's self-perceptions and possibly feedback from the coach.

In the third phase the coach encourages the coachee to generate different options or choices about their future actions. The coach as part of this process may ask the coachee to evaluate the different options as a way to help the coachee to become more aware of the implications of their possible choices.

In the final phase the coach asks the coachee to select one or more options and to summarize these as a plan of action.

At each stage the coach aims to facilitate the coachee through non-directive interventions, first to become both more aware of themselves, their actions and the actions or reactions of others, and second, to enhance the personal responsibility of the coachee, to enable them to recognize that the only thing they can change in the situation is themselves.

So what?

The approach has spawned a host of similar models, which at their heart focus on incremental performance improvement through new learning and adjustment of individual behaviour.

Alongside these simple models are more sophisticated behavioural coaching frameworks (Skiffington and Zeus, 2003) which take many of the GROW concepts and integrate these with the evidence-based research from behaviourist traditions, around human learning and behaviour.

As these models have developed in sophistication they have started to add elements that take the model beyond its behavioural focus towards cognitive behavioural interventions that encourage the coach to recognize explicitly the links between thoughts, emotions and behaviour.

In general, there is limited evidence to confirm the efficacy of GROW as a model specifically, although there is growing evidence on the impact of coaching on human learning and change (Grant *et al*, 2010). However, wider psychological research provides adequate evidence of the importance of goal setting on motivation (Locke and Latham, 1990) and on adults observing and learning from others in social situations (Bandura, 1969).

What else?

The central weakness of the model is its strength. GROW's appeal is its simple four-stage universal structure. As a result, it could be argued that the model fails to offer the flexibility to respond to different situations. In this sense it's a one-size-fits-all model.

One specific area which it fails to consider explicitly, at least in its original form, is the role of emotions and cognition and the impact of these on individual behaviour or performance. These aspects are more fully integrated into cognitive behavioural models such as those offered in counselling by Aaron Beck (1967) and in coaching by Stephen Palmer and Michael Neenan (Palmer and Szymanska, 2007; Neenan, 2006). In these models a wider approach is adopted and the coach aims to enable the coachee to recognize the relationship between these aspects and their personal triggers.

A third argument against behavioural-based approaches such as GROW is that their goal nature excludes the potential to explore philosophical aspects of life. Thus GROW may be suited to working in goal-directed areas of sports or business, but may be less well suited to careers conversations, person–role fit or life-coaching conversations where other approaches such as the transpersonal or existential approaches may be more helpful (Whitmore and Einzig, 2006).

Leadership challenge

Develop a plan to use this model with your top three performers. After a couple of coaching conversations, teach them the GROW model to start using it to coach others.

More help

Key references

Whitmore, J (2002) *Coaching for Performance: Growing people, performance and purpose*, Nicholas Brealey, London

Alexander, G (2006) *Behavioural coaching: The GROW model*, in *Excellence in Coaching*, ed J Passmore, Kogan Page, London

Other references

Bandura, A (1969) Social-learning theory of identificatory processes, in *Handbook of Socialization Theory and Research*, ed D A Goslin, pp 213–62, Rand McNally, Chicago

Beck, A T (1967) *Depression: Clinical, experimental and theoretical aspects*, University of Pennsylvania Press, Philadelphia

Grant, A M, Passmore, J, Cavanagh, M *et al* (2010) The state of play in coaching, *International Review of Industrial and Organizational Psychology*, 25, pp 125–68

Locke, E and Latham, G (1990) *A Theory of Goal Setting and Task Performance*, Prentice-Hall, Englewood Cliffs, NJ

Neenan, M (2006) Cognitive behavioural coaching, in *Excellence in Coaching*, ed J Passmore, Kogan Page, London

Palmer, S and Szymanska, K (2007) Cognitive behavioural coaching, in *The Handbook of Coaching Psychology*, ed S Palmer and A Whybrow, Routledge, Hove

Skiffington, S and Zeus, P (2003) *Behavioural Coaching: How to build sustainable personal and organizational strength*, McGraw-Hill, North Ryde, NSW

Whitmore, J and Einzig, H (2006) Transpersonal coaching, in *Excellence in Coaching*, ed J Passmore, Kogan Page, London

05

How can people learn to become more optimistic?

Learned optimism

The big idea

Learned optimism is the idea that people can develop the state of being optimistic just as they can develop any other talent, if they want to. To do this they need to encourage a habit of challenging any negative or pessimistic thought that enters the mind. As people practise this routine, over time they will learn how to become increasingly optimistic in response to circumstances.

Professor Martin Seligman, a prominent psychologist and one of the founders of the positive psychology movement, first offered this theory in his book *Learned Optimism* (Seligman, 1990). The theory developed out of Seligman's long-standing research interest in human helplessness. This, he says, is the state of mind where you believe that nothing you do can affect what actually happens to you. It is the mindset at the core of pessimism. Helplessness is a state that is learned rather than an unchangeable aspect of human nature or personality.

To become familiar with the principles underpinning learned optimism, Seligman encourages people to first understand learned helplessness. The two constructs are closely related, one almost mirroring the other. In his studies on helplessness in the 1960s Seligman and his colleagues found that a high percentage of the dogs they were using in behavioural research learned how to become helpless in the face of unpleasant conditions. Some did not, however, and managed to find a way out of their circumstances. Later experiments involving humans found that those people who felt they had a degree of control over their circumstances were less prone to helplessness even when they chose not to exercise that control (Hiroto and Seligman, 1975).

The work of Seligman and his colleagues progressed to try to establish why different people reacted with either pessimism or optimism when the circumstances ostensibly seemed to be the same. Their conclusion is that a shift to one or the other hinges on an individual's explanatory style. People who have a pessimistic explanatory style will interpret negative events as permanent, personal and pervasive. They might say, for example, 'If anything can go wrong it will always go wrong with me!' On the other hand, a person with an optimistic explanatory style will interpret negative events as passing blips, not spoiling the wider enjoyment of life and probably caused by some temporary problem that will be rectified. They might say, therefore, in contrast to the pessimist, 'I always try to look on the positive side after a setback and to the good things I know the future holds for me!'

So what?

To support the practical application of the theory, Seligman and colleagues developed two specific tools. The first is the Attributional Style Questionnaire (ASQ) and its derivatives. The ASQ presents 12 hypothetical events, half good and half bad. People are asked to write down the one major cause of each event and then rate the cause along a seven-point continuum for each of the three causal dimensions, permanence, pervasiveness and personalization. The ASQ provides a baseline measure of optimism. There is evidence that the ASQ is a predictor of depression, physical health, and achievement in various domains (Maruta *et al*, 2000; Sweeney, Anderson and Bailey, 1986).

If a person's ASQ reading is towards the pessimistic end of the spectrum, they can choose the second tool to help develop optimism. The person learns how to talk themselves through a situation in which they feel they are becoming pessimistic. This is a form of cognitive therapy. The structure follows an easy-to-remember acronym, ABCDE:

Adversity – what is the actual situation that is happening to you?

Belief – what are you thinking about the experience?

Consequence – how are you reacting emotionally and physically?

Disputation – reflect on how you might react differently to what is going on. Provide counter-evidence for any negative beliefs you are holding in your mind.

Energization – celebrate the successful disputation of negative beliefs and that you have been able to move forward.

Both of these tools have been used in a wide range of contexts. In the workplace the ASQ has been shown to be useful as a recruitment tool, enabling people with already high levels of optimism to be selected for jobs such as sales positions that require a quick bounce-back emotionally after a failed pitch (Schulman, 1999). The ABCDE tool has similarly been found to help people in high-pressure jobs build their capacity for optimism (Green, Medlin and Whitten, 2004; O'Grady, 2006). Some organizational development practitioners see plenty of unrealized potential to apply the theory and practices of learned optimism to both organizational culture and leadership styles (Danforth, 2009).

What else?

The topic of optimism is a broad one and the subject of considerable debate among psychologists, philosophers and others from a range of academic disciplines. Professor Christopher Peterson offers an overview of the different perspectives while Dr Tali Sharot reviews recent evidence from the world of neuroscience that suggests optimism may be hard-wired in the human brain (Peterson, 2000; Sharot, 2011). Those who critique learned optimism tend to focus on how the ASQ distinguishes and defines explanatory styles, although its validity and reliability as a test are generally accepted (Peterson, Buchanan and Seligman, 1995).

Leadership challenge

Complete the ASQ online and reflect on the results. What does this tell you about your own leadership practice? How can you develop a stronger optimistic approach within your team?

More help

A free online ASQ is available at: **http://www.optimistica.com/test.php**.

Key reference

Seligman, M E P (1990) *Learned Optimism: The skill to conquer life's obstacles, large and small*, Random House, New York

Other references

Danforth, S G (2009) *Optimistic Culture and Leadership*, Positive Leadership Dynamics, Wellesley, MA

Green Jr, K W, Medlin, B and Whitten, D (2004) Developing optimism to improve performance: an approach for the manufacturing sector, *Industrial Management and Data Systems*, **104** (2), pp 106–14

Hiroto, D S and Seligman, M E (1975) Generality of learned helplessness in man, *Journal of Personality and Social Psychology*, **31** (2), pp 311–27

Maruta, T, Colligan, R C, Malinchoc, M *et al* (2000) Optimists vs pessimists: survival rate among medical patients over a 30-year period, *Mayo Clinic Proceedings*, **75** (2), pp 140–3

O'Grady, C G (2006) Cognitive optimism and professional pessimism in the large-firm practice of law: the optimistic associate, *Law and Psychology Review*, **30**, pp 23–55

Peterson, C (2000) The future of optimism, *American Psychologist*, **55** (1), pp 44–55

Peterson, C, Buchanan, G and Seligman, M (1995) *Explanatory Style and Health*, Erlbaum, Hillsdale, NJ

Schulman, P (1999) Applying learned optimism to increase sales productivity, *Journal of Personal Selling and Sales Management*, **19**, pp 31–8

Sharot, T (2011) The optimism bias, *Time*, **177** (23), pp 40–6

Sweeney, P D, Anderson, K and Bailey, S (1986) Attributional style in depression: a meta-analytic review, *Journal of Personality and Social Psychology*, **50** (5), pp 974–91

06

Why did they do that?
Attribution theory

The big idea

At its very simplest, attribution theory is about how and why people explain events as they do. It's a theory of explanations! The theory looks at what sort of information people collect and how they use that information to explain why they think an event took place. Psychologist Fritz Heider (1896–1988) first developed attribution theory in his 1958 book *The Psychology of Interpersonal Relations*. Heider suggested that people see cause-and-effect relationships between people and events even when there may be none, and that this is what usually happens in life. Everyone, he says, is a naïve psychologist analysing everyone else (Heider, 1958).

He went on to propose that people, once they have observed or experienced an event, divide their explanations into two categories, external and internal. For a faulty action on their part they more often blame external factors, or 'She made me do it!' or 'It was the faulty equipment that slowed down my work rate.' On the other hand, when they are asked to explain other people's behaviours they are likely to blame a person's characteristics or lack of skills and say something like 'She is a poor manager' or 'He has always been a lazy worker.' They explain other people's behaviour by assuming that there was some internal motivation or attribute for what they observed and they also presume that such behaviour can be controlled by the individual. Where a behaviour is attributed to an external cause, the person's reaction is due to the demands of the situation and they are, therefore, held less personally responsible.

Heider terms this tendency to pay greater attention to external attributes in our own case and take less account of circumstances when it's to do with other people's actions as 'fundamental attribution error'. We jump to the wrong conclusion!

Jones and Davis (1966) developed the theory further by proposing that people pay more attention to what they perceive to be intentional behaviour than unthinking behaviour and that this is used to help us predict what we think the person will do in the future. So, for example, if we think that a person has a choice or is perceived to have acted deliberately, we, as observers, are likely to conclude that this reaction is part of their personality and, therefore, more likely to be repeated.

Harold Kelley suggests that there are three types of information that prompt people to create such links between cause and effect. The first is consensus. If many people appear to react in a similar way in a similar set of circumstances, people are likely to assume that external influences rather than personality type have caused the behaviour. The second is distinctiveness. If the behaviour is perceived to be outside the norm, it is likely to be attributed to external causes; however, if it is perceived to fit into a general pattern, it will be assumed that the person alone is responsible. The third is consistency. Behaviour that is observed to be consistent is more likely to be attributed to internal causes than to external influences (Kelley, 1967).

So what?

We can readily see how attribution theory is likely to help explain how managers, if they are not very careful, can be tempted to make incorrect judgements about the reasons for the performance of others, and themselves. There is an argument that the way people attribute causes to events can be learned and, therefore, changed (Rotter, 1975). Where managers and staff develop a supportive environment giving them greater control over events, they are likely to attribute more outcomes to 'internal' factors. This then connects attribution theory with motivation theory. The two are often described together. Once a behaviour has been observed and attributed, the theory suggests that it is likely that this information will be used to predict behaviour in similar circumstances. Managers can, therefore, gather data about behaviour in their staff and adjust their own decisions to support positive, performance-enhancing behaviours in the future.

There are also links with the theory of learned helplessness, developed initially by the psychologist Martin Seligman, well known for his ideas about positive psychology. 'Learned helplessness' is the condition of a person, or animal, who has learned to behave helplessly even when there is an opportunity for them to change their own circumstances (Seligman, 1975).

Attribution theory as developed by Weiner suggests that there are three attributional style dimensions: globality/specificity, stability/instability and internality/externality. An individual's attributional style may well predict how they will react in certain circumstances and the likelihood, or otherwise, of their entering into a state of learned helplessness (Weiner, 1986). To find out your attributional style, free tests are available on the internet (see link below).

What else?

A critique of the theory is that it is reductionist in that it assumes that a clear cause-and-effect link can be drawn and that interpretations will be logical and highly rational. It also tends to assume that there are no other factors that have a bearing on the judgements we make about the behaviours of others. An alternative view is that people are generally self-serving and will always credit success to themselves and failure as the fault of others. A meta-analysis of 500 studies by Mezulis *et al* (2004) found that self-serving attitudes do not vary between racial or gender groups or for that matter across different cultures.

Some researchers argue that the 'fundamental attribution error' is, to a large extent, a Western idea because non-Western cultures are more likely to view external attributions as an explanation of behaviour rather than initially consider internal explanations (Masuda and Nisbett, 2001). Arnold (2005) also suggests that the ultimate attribution bias is our tendency to attribute good performance to our racial group with a focus on ability and effort, but good performance by another racial group is put down to an easy task or help from colleagues. Similar research has been undertaken with regard to the perceptions of male and female groups of managers, with similar findings (Garland and Price, 1977). These studies suggest that the attribution error has potential implications for organizations' equality and diversity policies.

In recent decades, attribution theorists have moved away from considering individualistic approaches and are focusing more on shared patterns of attribution across groups.

Leadership challenge

Complete the free online attributional style questionnaire. What does this tell you about your own approach? How can you encourage your team to be more aware of their natural biases?

More help

Web material

Free attributional style questionnaire: **http://testyourself.psychtests.com/testid/2109**

Key references

Heider, F (1958) *The Psychology of Interpersonal Relations*, Wiley, New York

Jones, E E, Kanouse, D E, Kelley, H H *et al* (eds) (1972) *Attribution: Perceiving the causes of behavior*, General Learning Press, Morristown, NJ

Kelley, H H (1972) Attribution in social interaction, in *Attribution: Perceiving the causes of behavior*, ed E E Jones, D E Kanouse, H H Kelley *et al*, General Learning Press, Morristown, NJ

Weiner, B (1986) *An Attributional Theory of Motivation and Emotion*, Springer-Verlag, New York

Other references

Arnold, J (2005) *Work Psychology: Understanding human behaviour in the workplace*, 4th edn, Pearson Education, Harlow

Garland, H and Price, K H (1977) Attitudes toward women in management and attributions for their success and failure in a managerial position, *Journal of Applied Psychology*, **62** (1), pp 29–33

Jones, E E and Davis, K E (1966) From acts to dispositions: the attribution process in person perception, *Advances in Experimental Social Psychology*, **2**, pp 219–66

Kelley, H H (1967) Attribution theory in social psychology, in *Nebraska Symposium on Motivation*, vol 15, ed D Levine, pp 192–238, University of Nebraska Press, Lincoln

Masuda, T and Nisbett, R E (2001) Attending holistically vs. analytically: comparing the context sensitivity of Japanese and Americans, *Journal of Personality and Social Psychology*, **81**, pp 922–34

Mezulis, A H, Abramson, L Y, Hyde, J S *et al* (2004) Is there a universal positivity bias in attributions? A meta-analytic review of individual, developmental, and cultural differences in self-serving attributional bias, *Psychological Bulletin*, **130** (5), pp 711–47

Rotter, J B (1975) Some problems and misconceptions related to the construct of internal versus external control of reinforcement, *Journal of Consulting and Clinical Psychology*, **43** (1), pp 56–67

Seligman, M E P (1975) *Helplessness: On depression, development, and death*, W H Freeman, San Francisco

07

How can we make sense of who we are?

Personality trait and type theory

The big idea

Personality questionnaires try to help us understand ourselves or others better. Over the past four decades psychologists have developed hundreds of questionnaires which explore different aspects of personality. The most popular include 16PF, Saville Wave, the Myers–Briggs Type Indicator (MBTI), OPQ32, the Type Dynamics Indicator (TDI), the Margerison–McCann Team Management Profile and the NEO Five Factor Inventory. These questionnaires can be divided into two categories: those adopting a trait approach to personality and those adopting a type approach to personality.

A trait is a tendency in a person to act or react in a particular way. It can be a thought, feeling or action. So, for example, we might describe Ray as an anxious person. He might not be anxious all the time but we perceive him as someone who, in certain situations, seems anxious. He displays an anxiety trait. Allport classified traits as *Cardinal*, those which are core to a person, *Central*, those which distinguish one person from another, and *Secondary*, those which are relatively weak in a person. He saw them combining together to form the unique character of each person (Allport and Allport, 1921). Cattell, another very influential trait theorist, separated out what he called *surface* from *source* traits (Cattell, 2009). Surface traits are behaviour patterns seen by everyone day to day, while source traits are lifelong aspects of personality. He is most well known for designing the 16PF (Personality Factors) Questionnaire. Others have followed this model, including OPQ32 and Saville Wave. Almost all of these models have a core of five common meta-factors, commonly known as OCEAN – the 'Big Five' factors are openness, conscientiousness, extraversion, agreeableness and neuroticism.

The Big Five factor approach has come to dominate personality type research. With trait questionnaires the focus is on how much of this trait a person has. This is usually measured by a sten score, ie 1–10. As a result of this measurement these instruments are increasingly used for recruitment, as well as in personal development (Costa, McCrae and Psychological Assessment Resources, 1985).

In contrast, type theory focuses on given factors, which the individual either has or does not have. The most common of these type questionnaires is the MBTI, but others include TDI and the Margerison–McCann Team Management Profile.

So what?

Given the possibility of recruiting staff who have traits that match job requirements, it's not surprising that a huge amount has been written about how personality traits fit with the world of work. Furnham (1992) has identified no fewer than six different approaches to looking at this topic, ranging from classic personality theory to personality testing at work. It's the latter that has become well known in recent years.

Personality testing is controversial for some experts who say that people can fake the results, the tests are invalid anyway and can't really measure what they say they can. On the other hand, those in favour argue that it's very powerful to have some apparently quantifiable measures against key personality traits rather than relying on vague references from a previous employer. They also say that modern tests are very comprehensive in what they measure and have been rigorously tested. Certainly many employers have bought that argument and routinely use tests like the 16PF, the NEO-PI, and Saville and Holdsworth's Occupational Personality Questionnaire (OPQ), among others, in their recruitment and staff development processes. With the growing use of online tests, this is trend is likely to grow in the future as organizations use tests to screen applicants.

Personality type questionnaires such as the MBTI are not suitable for recruitment purposes, given that preference does not equate to competence. However, they do add value in personal and leadership development activities, where they help people gain a better sense of their personality preferences and how these can impact on others, and provide a common language with which to talk about these within their team.

What else?

The growth of the personality questionnaire has been matched by the decline in substantial criticism of such instruments. There are those who say that the simplicity of the models ignores the complexity of human behaviour, or that human behaviour has a strong situational component. Alongside this is a view that they do not really measure what they say they do. Just because a person has a particular trait does not mean that their behaviour in any given situation is predictable.

Furnham acknowledges that not all personality dimensions are equal when it comes to assessing suitability for different types of work. It is important to relate specific traits to specific work outcomes for the measures to be of value (Furnham, 2005).

Of course, success in a role is not down solely to the individual personality characteristics of the employee but also to the organizational culture within which they are expected to perform.

Leadership challenge

Compete a personality questionnaire, such as the TDI (with a licensed facilitator). Think about your personality and how this impacts on your leadership style. What changes would you like to make to lead different members of your team more effectively?

More help

TDI website: **http://www.teamfocus.co.uk/tests-and-questionnaires/ assessing-personality/type-dynamics-indicator.php**

Key reference

Furnham, A (2005) *The Psychology of Behaviour at Work: The individual in the organization*, Psychology Press, Hove, Sussex

Other references

Allport, F H and Allport, G W (1921) Personality traits: their classification and measurement, *Journal of Abnormal Psychology and Social Psychology*, **16** (1), pp 6–40

Cattell, R B (2009) *The Scientific Analysis of Personality*, Transaction Publishers, Piscataway, NJ

Costa, P T, McCrae, R R and Psychological Assessment Resources (1985) *The NEO Personality Inventory: Manual, form S and form R*, Psychological Assessment Resources, Odessa, FL

Furnham, A (1992) Personality and learning style: a study of three instruments, *Personality and Individual Differences*, **13** (4), pp 429–38

How does psychological testing work?

08

Psychometrics

The big idea

Psychometrics is the term used to refer to a broad range of assessments and measures of intelligence, aptitude and personality (McKenna, 2006). Sometimes the term is used interchangeably with the phrase 'psychological testing', while some psychologists prefer to define psychometrics as the science that underpins the testing process. Either way, the use of psychometrics continues to have a high profile across a wide range of domains, including business, education, people and organizational development, mental health and the rehabilitation of brain-injured patients.

Historical background

Sir Francis Galton, a cousin of Charles Darwin, is credited with pioneering the first psychometric questionnaire in the late 19th century (Galton, 1961). His ideas led ultimately to the development of the first tests of intelligence by Alfred Binet (Binet, Simon and Town, 1913). The first couple of decades of the 20th century saw the development of methodologies for assessing intelligence. Binet's work eventually became known as the Intelligence Quotient (IQ). From the 1920s to 1940 testing for different personality types became the major interest of many psychologists. The outbreak of the Second World War, with the need to make the most of scarce labour, saw a demand from employers and the military for ways of measuring job aptitude and ability. Psychologists responded by developing relevant practical tests.

In recent years the trend has been to apply psychological testing, and personality testing in particular, through internet-based tools to ever-widening areas of life.

Characteristics of psychological tests

A psychological test usually has three main characteristics:

1 It seeks to record a sample of behaviour at a given point in time. People are required to do something, often responding to questions or making choices between a set of alternatives. To be valid a test must demonstrably measure the behaviours it claims to be measuring.

2 The sample is obtained under standardized conditions. Such conditions are important because a psychological test measures a person's performance relative to other people. Everyone sitting a test should therefore ideally have the same physical conditions and time to complete it. Standardization also enables the tester to better judge if the test is reliable. If it can be repeated with similar results then it is reliable.

3 There are established scoring rules to obtain quantitative information from the sample. The aim is to ensure that as much objectivity as possible is built into the way the tests are marked. This enhances reliability and enables fair comparisons to be made between individuals. Raw scores are consolidated and, using statistical tools, norms are established. These are the ranges of scores obtained from a large representative group which can then be used to compare the performance of individuals.

There are a number of tests which are also included in the broad family of psychometrics but whose measurement characteristics differ from those above. They include:

1 Specific task performance tests which challenge the person to exert maximal effort in a given situation.

2 Observations of a person's behaviour within a particular context. An example of this is observed group work in a leadership assessment centre.

3 Self-report measures which invite people to describe their feelings and attitudes. Many personality inventories are like this.

So what?

In a business context, personality tests particularly have gained widespread popularity. Employers make assumptions that intelligence has been tested through the education system. Their concerns are now primarily focused on selecting and ultimately promoting people with the right personality who 'fit' the job and the organization. This trend has prompted strong debate about the merits of these tests among both psychologists and non-psychologists. Positively, personality tests are seen by some as:

- providing quantitative data to compare people against agreed criteria;
- offering a scientific, reliable basis for differentiating between people;
- comprehensive and fair;
- a source of data that can be kept for comparison and measurement at a later date.

Other people consider them unreliable because:

- People may not have sufficient self-awareness to answer the questions accurately.
- Questions may be misread or people deliberately set out to give a false impression.
- Tests of this type rarely actually measure what they say they are measuring. They have a weak validity.
- Questions can be biased towards different racial and gender groups, as some tests do not allow for cultural differences.
- There are no good norms against which to assess personalities.
- The evidence base that links personality test scores with actual performance in a job is relatively weak.

(McKenna, 2006)

There are a number of practical and ethical issues surrounding the use of all types of psychological test. Every test should include a supporting manual that details the scientific data confirming its validity and reliability. Those administering tests and providing feedback to subjects need to be well trained. Maintaining security of test papers and confidentiality of results is vital if the status of a test is not to be undermined. Tests should be used for the purpose for which they were designed. Employers can be tempted to over-rely on test results when making judgements about selection or promotion.

What else?

The literature on psychometrics contains detailed research and critique on most widely available tests. On the broader debate about the usefulness or otherwise of testing, the jury is divided. Some, like Ghiselli (1973), believe that they have some value in personnel selection. Others, like Blinkhorn (1997), have little faith in their usefulness. There is a general view that the discipline of psychometrics will be strengthened if it puts more effort into incorporating recent advances in knowledge about human behaviour in tests and assessment processes. Without doing so, it risks being locked into an outdated set of assumptions and becoming less useful to business as a consequence (McKenna, 2006).

Leadership challenge

What role can psychometrics play in helping you to develop yourself and your team?

More help

Key reference

McKenna, E F (2006) *Business Psychology and Organizational Behaviour*, 4th edn, Psychology Press, Hove, Sussex

Other references

Binet, A, Simon, T and Town, C H (1913) *A Method of Measuring the Development of the Intelligence of Young Children*, Courier, Lincoln, IL

Blinkhorn, S (1997) Past imperfect, future conditional: fifty years of test theory, *British Journal of Mathematical and Statistical Psychology*, 50, pp 175–85

Galton, S F (1961) *Classification of Men according to their Natural Gifts*, Hayes Barton Press, Raleigh, NC

Ghiselli, E E (1973) The validity of aptitude tests in personnel selection, *Personnel Psychology*, 26 (4), pp 461–77

How do we think about others thinking?

Theory of mind and emotional intelligence

The big idea

The theory of mind (ToM) is the ability to attribute mental states, such as beliefs and emotions, to oneself and to others. This ability to think about our thinking, often commonly called reflection, and to think about others has been a key factor in humans' success. Arguably it has helped us improve our cooperation with others in the group, as well as enhance our learning.

ToM appears to be innate to humans, but its development seems to take years to mature, reaching different levels of maturity in different people. One key aspect is empathy. Empathy is the ability to put ourselves mentally in someone else's shoes; to 'see their world as if it were our own'. Recent research with other species suggests that humans are not alone in showing an understanding of others' emotions; even rodents may exhibit empathic abilities (de Waal, 2007).

One of the most important milestones in an individual's development of their personal ToM is the ability to attribute 'false belief' to others. This is the ability to recognize that others can have beliefs which are different from our own and that such beliefs will reflect an individual's knowledge and experiences; and further, that understanding such beliefs can help us understand that person's behaviour in different situations.

While research and development of ToM have concentrated on child development, the concept has been foundational in the development of emotional intelligence – often described as EQ (emotional quotient).

Howard Gardner first offered the idea of multiple intelligences, among which he included both interpersonal intelligence (the capacity to understand the thoughts and feelings of other people) and intrapersonal intelligence (the

FIGURE 9.1 Emotional intelligence

Understanding our own emotions

Understanding others' emotions

Adapting our behaviour to
achieve the outcome we want

capacity to understand one's own thoughts and feelings) (Gardner, 1983). This has subsequently been developed by writers such as Reuven Bar-On and Peter Salovey.

Emotional intelligence (EI) broadly has three components: to understand one's own emotions, to understand the emotions of others and to adjust our behaviour appropriately to achieve a desired outcome (Figure 9.1).

Various models and definitions have been proposed and there continues to be wide-ranging debate about the application and value of EI and how to measure it (see, for example, Passmore, Tong and Wildflower, 2011).

So what?

The concept of thinking about our thinking and thinking about others' thinking has immense value in a connected world. In the workplace, managers need to influence others to undertake complex tasks, often remotely. Consultants and coaches need to judge where their client is in order to provide the next question or advice, to take them forward. Just reflecting on the idea and what we think and what others think is likely to heighten our self-awareness and our impact on others.

A number of researchers and psychologists have worked to develop this general concept into a model they can apply to help others develop. This has led to the development of a host of psychological questionnaires (psychometrics) which claim to measure an individual's level of EI. These questionnaires can largely be divided into two schools: ability-based questionnaires such as the Mayer–Salovey–Caruso Emotional Intelligence Test (MSCEIT) and self-evaluation questionnaires such as EQ-i.

Salovey and Mayer's conception of EI defines EI as 'The ability to perceive emotion, integrate emotion to facilitate thought, understand emotions and to regulate emotions to promote personal growth' (Mayer *et al*, 2001). The ability-based model views emotions as useful sources of information which can help managers and others to make sense of, and navigate, the social environment in the workplace and wider world. The model proposes that individuals vary in their ability to process information of an emotional nature and in their ability to relate emotional processing to a wider cognition. This ability is seen to manifest itself in certain adaptive behaviours. The model claims that EI includes four types of abilities:

1 perceiving emotions – the ability to detect and decipher emotions in faces, pictures, voices and art – including the ability to identify one's own emotions;

2 using emotions – the ability to use emotions to facilitate various cognitive activities, such as thinking and problem solving;

3 understanding emotions – the ability to comprehend emotional language and to appreciate complicated relationships among emotions;

4 managing emotions – the ability to regulate emotions in both ourselves and in others. Therefore, the emotionally intelligent person can harness emotions, even negative ones, and manage them to achieve intended goals.

More recently, Salovey has gone on to offer insights into how managers can build their emotional competences (Caruso and Salovey, 2004, 2008). This includes guidance on getting into the right mood for the task in hand, as well as becoming more attuned to one's emotional state.

The alternative to the ability-based questionnaires is self-report questionnaires such as the Bar-On Emotional Quotient Inventory (EQ-i). The EQ-i does not measure personality traits or capacity, but rather the mental ability to be successful in dealing with environmental demands and pressures. In contrast to Salovey's four-element model, Bar-On's has five main components, which have echoes from Gardner's original multiple intelligences. The five components are: intrapersonal, interpersonal, stress management, adaptability, and general mood/happiness. In this sense the model seems to combine ideas from EI with ideas offered by Seligman and Fredrickson, such as learned optimism and the broaden-and-build theory (discussed elsewhere in this book), which identify optimistic emotional states as important elements in human functioning.

What else?

Criticisms of EQ have centred on whether the construct is a real intelligence in the way in which IQ operates. This debate continues. Secondly, there has been considerable debate about the various attempts to measure it through questionnaires. The EI ability model has been criticized in the research for lacking face validity (see page 79) and predictive validity in the workplace – for example, questions include emotional responses to the image of a tree in a desert. The EQ-i has been found to be highly susceptible to faking (Day and Carroll, 2008).

These debates continue and reflect both commercial and academic interests in this emerging field. Despite these debates, the idea of ToM and its application through ideas such as EI have value for leaders and those working in organizations. At the heart of these is the idea that we reflect on our thinking and emotions to regulate our behaviour and optimize our performance at work.

Leadership challenge

Think about the last time you were angry with someone. What did you do? Was your behaviour a 'reaction' (driven by your emotions), or controlled to produce the desired result (taking account of the individual, their emotional state and the behaviour most likely to achieve your desired outcome)? What could you do differently next time to catch your emotions before they hijack your behaviour? What options have you got as to how you behave? (You can't set a plan for this, as you don't know the situation, how the other person will be feeling or what behaviours might suit the situation.)

More help

Key references

Caruso, D and Salovey, P (2004) *The Emotionally Intelligent Manager: How to develop and use the four key emotional skills of leadership*, Wiley, San Francisco

Passmore, J, Tong, C and Wildflower, L (2011) Theories of intelligence, in *The Handbook of Knowledge-Based Coaching: What we really do when we coach*, ed D Brennan and L Wildflower, Wiley, New York

Other references

Bar-On, R and Parker, J D A (2000) *The Handbook of Emotional Intelligence: Theory, development, assessment, and application at home, school, and in the workplace*, Jossey-Bass, San Francisco

Caruso, D and Salovey, P (2008) Coaching for emotional intelligence: MSCEIT, in *Psychometrics in Coaching*, ed J Passmore, Kogan Page, London

Day, A L and Carroll, S A (2008) Faking emotional intelligence (EI): comparing response distortion on ability and trait-based EI measures, *Journal of Organizational Behavior*, **29**, pp 761–84

de Waal, F B M (2007) Commiserating mice, *Scientific American*, 24 June

Gardner, H (1983) *Frames of Mind*, Basic Books, New York

Mayer, J D, Salovey, P, Caruso, D L *et al* (2001) Emotional intelligence as a standard intelligence, *Emotion*, **1**, pp 232–42

Perks, J and Bar-On, R (2010) Coaching for emotionally intelligent leadership, in *Leadership coaching*, ed J Passmore, Kogan Page, London

Salovey, P and Mayer, J D (1990) Emotional intelligence, *Imagination, Cognition, and Personality*, **9**, pp 185–211

How can we manage our negative thinking?

Cognitive behavioural model

The big idea

The earliest expression of the cognitive behavioural approach can be traced back to the first century AD when a Stoic philosopher, Epictetus, observed how people 'are not disturbed by things but by the view they take of them'. Much later, in the 18th century, another philosopher, Kant, described the four consecutive steps from perception to action: 'I see a tiger; I think I'm in danger; I feel afraid; I run.' In this short set of four statements Kant highlighted the link between the human cognition, emotion and behaviour, and illustrated that humans make use of cognitions and emotions in each decision for action.

More recently, the information-processing model has argued that during periods of stress or high demand a person's thinking becomes more rigid and distorted. As a result, judgement and decision making deteriorate and the individual's basic beliefs about themselves and others become fixed.

The cognitive perspective was also highlighted by the psychiatrist Alfred Adler. He observed that people determine themselves by the meaning they give to situations (Adler, 1958). Albert Ellis further developed these ideas. He explored the mechanics of emotional disturbance, which later became known as rational emotive behaviour therapy (Ellis, 1962). He observes the intermediary role beliefs play between an activating event and a person's emotional and behavioural responses. The ideas were later developed for use by leaders and others in organizations (Ellis, 1972).

Aaron Beck further developed the value of the cognitive model through his cognitive therapy model (Beck, 1967, 1976). This placed the emphasis on the role of 'internal dialogue' (Beck, 1976). He argued that individuals' subsequent feelings and behaviour were informed by their thoughts (or inner voice). Beck found that while clients were not always conscious of their internal voice, they could learn to identify it. Once it had been identified, they were then in a position to examine any automatic, emotion-filled thoughts and, where useful, replace them with an alternative voice which was both more performance enhancing and more based on evidence.

So what?

The model, which was developed initially in philosophy and later adopted and developed by counsellors such as Adler, Beck and Ellis, has implications for those who work in coaching and development, as well as for leaders.

A host of more organizational friendly models have been developed for application in workplace settings (Palmer and Williams, in press). A selection of these models is summarized in Table 10.1.

TABLE 10.1 Organizational friendly cognitive models

Cognitive behavioural models	Model steps
The PRACTICE model (Palmer, 2007)	**P**roblem identification; **R**ealistic, relevant goals developed; **A**lternative solution(s) generated; **C**onsideration of consequence; **T**arget most feasible solution(s); **I**mplementation of **C**hosen solution(s); **E**valuation
The SPACE model (Edgerton and Palmer, 2005)	**S**ocial context; **P**hysiology; **A**ction; **C**ognition; **E**motion
ACE FIRST model (Lee, 2003)	**A**ctions; **C**ognitions; **E**motions; and **F**ocus; **I**ntentions; **R**esults; **S**ystem; **T**ension
The CRAIC model (O'Donovan, 2009)	**C**ontrol; **R**esponsibility; **A**wareness; **I**mpetus; **C**onfidence
The INTENT model (Good, Yeganeh and Yeganeh, 2009)	**I**deal future; **N**ow; **T**argeted cognitions and behaviours; **E**xperiment; **N**urture; **T**ransition

At the heart of each of these models is a focus on helping individuals to recognize the relationship between their thoughts, feelings and behaviour, to develop a more evidenced-based approach and to move from performance-inhibiting thinking to performance-enhancing thinking (Neenan and Palmer, 2012). The models typically follow the core ABCDE framework:

- Exploring activating events – what triggers the feeling or thoughts?
- Exploring beliefs – what thoughts come to mind for the individual when discussing the situation and individuals involved? What core beliefs underpin these thoughts?
- What are the consequences of these beliefs? What does the individual do or how do they behave in the situation or with these individuals?
- What disputing evidence can the individual call upon to challenge these beliefs? What techniques or tools can the individual or their coach offer to help them cope or manage in the situation more effectively?
- What effective outlook will help them into the future? What worldview can the person develop for themselves to use in future situations?

Such ideas have value in a wide variety of ways for coaches as well as for consultants and leaders in organizations.

What else?

The central weakness of the cognitive behavioural model is that it downplays the aspects of the unconscious and fails to deal adequately with client resistance or readiness for change. Psychodynamic and systemic models draw attention to issues which may be outside the awareness of the individual but can be driving or influencing behaviour at both an individual and an organization level. An equally serious concern is that the model pays limited attention to the individual's readiness for change and how the change manager can work with the individual or organization to help them make progress towards a position where they are ready, willing and able to engage in a change process. Once in this place, cognitive behavioural therapy (CBT) and other cognitive approaches offer a useful model for helping both individuals and organizations forward towards their desired goal (see Anstiss and Passmore, 2012 for a full discussion of change readiness preparations within a CBT context).

Leadership challenge

Think about a new challenge approaching in the next three months which makes you anxious or is taking your mental energy thinking about it. Think about the following five questions and how you can help your thinking move from performance-inhibiting thinking to performance-enhancing thinking:

1 What feelings about the challenge come to mind?
2 What thoughts come to mind when you think about the challenge?

3 What evidence is there to draw on to support these initial thoughts?

4 How helpful are these thoughts in optimizing your performance?

5 What changes could you make to your thoughts which might contribute to an improvement in your performance at this event? (Try to think of a new saying which you can say to yourself and that will help you feel more confident.)

More help

Key reference

Neenan, M (2006) Cognitive behavioural coaching, in *Excellence in Coaching*, ed J Passmore, Kogan Page, London

Other references

Adler, A (1958) *What Life Should Mean to You*, ed A Porter, Capricorn, New York (originally published 1931)

Anstiss, T and Passmore, J (2012) Motivational interview, in *Cognitive Behavioural Coaching in Practice: An evidence based approach*, ed M Neenan and S Palmer, pp 33–52, Routledge, London

Beck, A T (1967) *Depression: Clinical, experimental, and theoretical aspects*, University of Pennsylvania Press, Philadelphia

Beck, A T (1976) *Cognitive Therapy and the Emotional Disorders*, New American Library, New York

Edgerton, N and Palmer, S (2005) SPACE: a psychological model for use within cognitive behavioural coaching, therapy and stress management, *The Coaching Psychologist*, 2 (2), pp 25–31

Ellis, A (1962) *Reason and Emotion in Psychotherapy*, Lyle Stuart, New York

Ellis, A (1972) *Executive Leadership: A rational approach*, Institute for Rational-Emotive Therapy, New York

Good, D, Yeganeh, R and Yeganeh, B (2009) *Cognitive Behavioral Executive Coaching: A generative merging of practices*, Academy of Management Annual Meeting, Chicago

Lee, G (2003) *Leadership Coaching: From personal insight to organizational performance*, CIPD, London

Neenan, M and Palmer, S (eds) (2012) *Cognitive Behavioural Coaching in Practice: An evidence based approach*, pp 33–52, Routledge, London

O'Donovan, H (2009) CRAIC – a model suitable for Irish coaching psychology, *The Coaching Psychologist*, 5 (2), pp 90–6

Palmer, S (2007) PRACTICE: A model suitable for coaching, counselling, psychotherapy and stress management, *The Coaching Psychologist*, 3 (2), pp 71–7

Palmer, S and Williams, H (in press) Cognitive behavioural coaching, in *The Wiley-Blackwell Handbook of the Psychology of Coaching and Mentoring*, ed J Passmore, D Peterson and T Freire, Wiley-Blackwell, Oxford

How can job performance be accurately and fairly assessed?

11

Behaviourally anchored rating scales (BARS)

The big idea

Behaviourally anchored rating scales (BARS) connect specific behaviours in a job with a performance rating (Smith and Kendall, 1963). Instead of someone being assessed in a job as poor, average or excellent by the arbitrary judgement of a manager, BARS requires that they are rated against a set of pre-agreed observable behaviours related to the performance of the job. The scales usually run from 1 to 5, where 1 is an unsatisfactory performance, defined by the absence of a key behaviour, through to exceptional performance at the top end. The types of behaviour vary according to the elements within a specific job. So, for example, a leadership development facilitator who struggles to be audible during a session will be rated at the lower end of the scale, while someone who communicates loudly, clearly and logically would be assessed at a higher rating. Each job will have its own BARS.

Creating BARS is a four-step process:

1 A group of employees and managers, who understand the job in detail and who are highly rated (subject matter experts or SMEs), meet and define the factors and behaviours that are needed to perform the job effectively. They will be helped by data gathered from task and critical incident analysis (critical incident analysis asks people to tell the story of an incident that made a positive or negative

impact on the achievement of a task). Key behaviours and activities are highlighted by the group, who then convert them into job performance dimensions.

2 A second group of SMEs provide examples of behaviours that match the job performance dimensions, giving an indication whether a behaviour indicates poor, average or excellent performance.

3 A third independent group of SMEs cross-matches the information from Step 2 with Step 1. If there is a high level of agreement between the experts, the behaviour is accepted; if not, it's discarded. Statistical techniques such as standard deviation can be used to help ensure that the behaviours with a high level of agreement are consistently retained.

4 The final set of agreed behaviours are set against the 1–5 scale and serve as 'behaviour anchors'. A BARS has been created.

So what?

Advantages

Assessing performance in a job can be a difficult process. BARS helps reduce employee uncertainty about what constitutes good performance by linking it with demonstrable behaviours. This means that there is clarity and an increased sense of fairness about the assessment process. Since BARS is meant to be applied across a whole company, jobs can be individually considered and this enhances transparency and fairness. BARS has the advantage of being easy to use by managers and more acceptable to employees than other methods of assessment. The scales are explicit about desired behaviours, so BARS helps the employee understand how they can improve performance.

Disadvantages

Developing BARS is a time-consuming and expensive process. Even though it's a rigorous process, some key behaviours can get left out, leading to complications for managers when assessing performance. Maintaining BARS is probably even more time-consuming than creating them in the first place. In fast-changing business environments where managers expect flexibility in job roles and behaviours, the pace of change can outstrip the resources to keep BARS updated.

What else?

Research about the value of BARS suggests that it may produce results only marginally more accurate than other methods of assessing performance

(Arnold and Randall, 2010; Jacobs, Kafry and Zedeck, 1980; Murphy and Constans, 1987). There are also questions about whether or not BARS really is that objective, given the preconceptions and biases of the SMEs designing the scales. That's a criticism of all human performance assessment methods but with BARS the question tends to be about whether or not it provides value for money. A counterargument is that you can minimize cost and effort if you combine the BARS process with job analysis (Arnold and Randall, 2010).

BARS has been used to define the behaviours of a subgroup within a whole profession (Grussing, Valuck and Williams, 1994) and helped clarify what, in behavioural terms, is meant by the phrase 'a learning organization' (Campbell and Cairns, 1994). These demonstrate in practice the flexible use of BARS.

Leadership challenge

With a colleague, redraft your role descriptions, describing them in behavioural and success terms. Using the insights of your colleague, put BARS against each of the performance dimensions.

More help

Key reference

Smith, P C and Kendall, L M (1963) Retranslation of expectations: an approach to the construction of unambiguous anchors for rating scales, *Journal of Applied Psychology*, **47** (2), pp 149–55

Other references

Arnold, J and Randall, R (2010) *Work Psychology: Understanding human behaviour in the workplace*, 5th edn, Pearson Education, Harlow

Campbell, T and Cairns, H (1994) Developing and measuring the learning organization: from buzz words to behaviours, *Industrial and Commercial Training*, **26** (7), pp 10–15

Grussing, P G, Valuck, R J and Williams, R G (1994) Development and validation of behaviorally-anchored rating scales for student evaluation of pharmacy instruction, *American Journal of Pharmaceutical Education*, **58** (1), pp 25–37

Jacobs, R, Kafry, D and Zedeck, S (1980) Expectations of behaviorally anchored rating scales, *Personnel Psychology*, **33** (3), pp 595–640

Murphy, K R and Constans, J I (1987) Behavioral anchors as a source of bias in rating, *Journal of Applied Psychology*, **72** (4), pp 573–7

12

How do people cope with change?

Phases of change models

The big idea

The work on the psychology of death and dying by physician Elisabeth Kubler-Ross continues to be hugely influential in shaping people's understanding, not just about dying, but also about organizational change (Kubler-Ross, 1969). In fact, her ideas are cited in any context where some shift in the attitudes and emotions surrounding change needs to take place.

Kubler-Ross observes that dying patients pass through five stages of grief as death approaches (Table 12.1).

TABLE 12.1   Kubler-Ross's stages of grief

Kubler-Ross stage	Explanation
1 Denial	Denial is the conscious or unconscious refusal to accept the facts of the situation. It can be understood as a natural defence mechanism which people use when dealing with a change that can, for a time, be ignored.
2 Anger	Anger can be directed inwards or towards others, especially to those close to the one experiencing loss. It can be expressed in many different ways.
3 Bargaining	This happens when individuals think they can avoid the loss, even death, by doing a deal with either God or another person. People seek some sort of compromise but this is often unlikely to be sustainable.

TABLE 12.1 *Continued*

Kubler-Ross stage	Explanation
4 Depression	At this stage people begin to accept the sadness of the situation in which they find themselves. It has been called 'preparatory grieving'.
5 Acceptance	This stage varies according to a person's situation but it does reflect a degree of emotional detachment and objectivity.

SOURCE: adapted from Kubler-Ross (1969) and **http://www.ekrfoundation.org/five-stages-of-grief**

The five stages are not intended to be interpreted as a process that everyone, albeit with different timings, goes through, but rather a framework or model. People, Kubler-Ross suggests, will not necessarily experience all the stages, nor will there be a clear differentiation between them. Transition between them may be more of an ebb and flow than a clear progression. This 'grief cycle' has been adopted as a process by those interested in change management and reinterpreted as a change curve (Figure 12.1).

FIGURE 12.1   The 'grief cycle' reinterpreted as a change curve

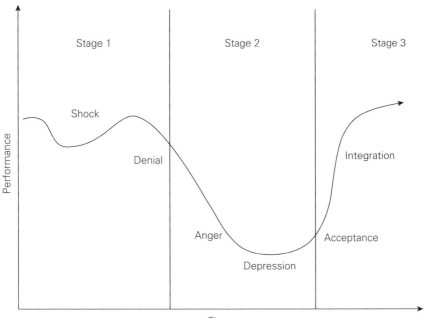

The five Kubler-Ross stages are compressed into three broad domains of experience and 'integration' added to indicate that performance following a change will always return to pre-change levels, or better. The tendency is to assume that all change will evoke similar feelings and that such a linear process is normal.

So what?

Colin Carnall's seven phases of change (Table 12.2) is one example of how the Kubler-Ross model has been used to illustrate the feelings and behaviours of people experiencing change in an organizational context (Carnall, 2007).

TABLE 12.2   Carnall's seven phases of change

Phase	Description
Shock and surprise	Faced with new information about business challenges, people realize that they can no longer continue with their old ways of working. There is some acknowledgement that they do not have the capabilities they need to see them through.
Denial and refusal	Core values reassert themselves, giving the feeling that change is not really necessary after all. People believe that their current competency is sufficient to see them through any challenge.
Rational understanding	Some recognition that maybe there is a case for change after all. The focus tends to be on finding short-term solutions rather than addressing more deep-seated ones, including the need for behavioural and attitudinal change.
Emotional acceptance	A critical point, where either management succeeds in convincing people of the case for change or change processes grind to a halt.
Exercising and learning	If people are convinced, they then start to try new behaviours and develop new processes. Some of these may fail but it is the change leader's responsibility to create some early wins. This builds confidence and motivation to move forward.
Realization	By reflecting on the learning from early changes, people understand better what works in the new context. They perceive that their competency is sufficient to perform well in the new environment.
Integration	New behaviours and attitudes become part of everyday routine.

SOURCE: adapted from Carnall (2007)

A web search reveals a huge range of similar models all based, to some extent, on the Kubler-Ross grief cycle, including, for example:

http://www.changecycle.com/changecycle.htm

http://onproductmanagement.net/2010/07/11/the-change-cycle/

http://changingminds.org/disciplines/chage_management/
     psychology_change/

Some acknowledge the source of their inspiration while others don't. These recent frameworks demonstrate the continuing widespread popularity among change managers and organizational consultants of a model that seems to offer a way of understanding the emotional and psychological aspects of change.

What else?

Perhaps somewhat surprising is the absence of any research that supports the Kubler-Ross grief cycle. Furthermore, psychologists working in the field of grief and grieving over the past two decades generally no longer use or reference the model. The consensus seems to be that while Elisabeth Kubler-Ross was a pioneer in her time, the framework is unsubstantiated, misinterpreted and simply assumed to be true. Use of the model in the popular media and by trainers has compounded this perception (Bonanno and Boerner, 2007; Hoy, 2011; Konigsberg, 2011). More recent research explores the nature of grief and offers new perspectives on people's experiences (Bonanno and Boerner, 2007). There is no evidence that supports the effectiveness of the many derivative 'change cycles' that are used in organizational contexts.

Leadership challenge

Think about a time when you have experienced significant change. How do these models fit with your experience? What are the lessons for the next change you lead?

More help

Key references

Kubler-Ross, E (1969) *On Death and Dying*, Macmillan, London
Carnall, C A (2007) *Managing Change in Organizations*, Pearson Education, Harlow

Other references

Bonanno, G A and Boerner, K (2007) The stage theory of grief, *Journal of the American Medical Association*, **297** (24), p 2693

Hoy, W G [accessed 28 September, 2011] Unveiling the 'myths' in the truth about grief [Online] http://griefconnect.com/Documents/The%20Myths%20of%20 the%20Truth%20about%20Grief.pdf

Konigsberg, R D (2011) *The Truth about Grief: The myth of its five stages and the new science of loss*, Simon & Schuster, New York

How do we understand different types of people?

Myers–Briggs Type Indicator (MBTI)

The big idea

The Myers–Briggs Type Indicator (MBTI) is a very well known and popular personality type questionnaire. It is used by coaches and people developers in a wide range of contexts to help individuals and teams better understand their personalities and differences. The tool measures the clarity of people's psychological preferences across a range of dimensions but with a focus on how they see the world and make decisions.

MBTI was developed by mother-and-daughter team Katherine Myers and Isabel Myers Briggs (Myers, 1962) who based their work on a psychological type theory originally developed by Carl Jung (Jung, 1923). His theory is that people can be divided into two basic types, extraverts and introverts. Jung is referring not to sociability but to how people direct their energies. An extravert is likely to look outwards to the environment while an introvert will gain energy through thoughts and experiences in their inner world. Jung built on his ideas and later added two pairs of opposite mental functions. Myers and Briggs called these Sensing–Intuition and Thinking–Feeling in their model and added a third pair of functions, Judging–Perceiving. This, they thought, better reflected the assumptions in Jung's original work.

Short definitions

The four dichotomies of the MBTI are listed in Table 13.1.

These dichotomies reflect preferences people have for thinking and behaving. Everyone can express each of the eight but, according to the theory, we all have a set of preferences we habitually use.

TABLE 13.1   The four dichotomies of the MBTI

Extraversion: Looks outward for energy	**I**ntroversion: Looks to own thoughts and experiences for energy
Sensing: Uses the five senses to understand the world	**In**tuition: Perceives patterns and relationships
Thinking: Logical and rational analysis of situations	**F**eeling: Understanding, empathy and social values
Judging: Decides by using one of the **T**hinking or **F**eeling processes	**P**erceiving: Decides by using one of the **S**ensing or **In**tuition processes

How it works

The MBTI is usually administered in two parts by a trained and accredited practitioner. The first part is a questionnaire containing 88 (93 in the US version) questions that prompt preference decisions. The second is an in-depth one-to-one conversation, using the results, to help a person to decide which combination of preferences best represents their way of 'being' in the world. The conversation will also cover some of the subtleties of the model, including a look at the dominant (leading) function and the auxiliary (balancing) functions. The end result is an agreed four-letter acronym, for example ENFJ, that best summarizes their personality type.

The licence to the model is now held by CPP Inc (**www.cpp.com**) who govern the production of materials, authorize trainers and update the *MBTI Manual* (Myers, 2003).

So what?

When using MBTI it's vital to recognize that it does not absolutely define who people are as personalities but gives an indication of people's preferences. The intention of Katherine Myers and Isabel Myers Briggs was that people would come to value the different characteristics of others and so find life, including working life, more satisfying (Myers and Myers, 1995). It's recommended that the indicator is always taken voluntarily and in confidence, giving the person the freedom to control if and how their preferences are shared. There are practical ways in which this can be respected while working with teams, who often find it very beneficial to share types with one another. Such a process, carefully facilitated, positively assists teams understand something of what makes each member tick.

It is also worth bearing in mind that, unlike tests for personality traits such as the 16PF and Saville Wave, the MBTI does not indicate an amount of type but the degree to which a preference is clear in the understanding of the person. It also does not measure ability, nor does it give an indication if someone will be good at a particular job. This last point is really important and means that companies are advised not to use the MBTI for staff recruitment or assessment for promotion.

While there are quite a few caveats around the use of the MBTI, many coaches and people developers report that it is a very valuable tool in deepening people's awareness of how they and their colleagues think, feel and act.

What else?

Much work has been done to ensure that the construction of the MBTI questionnaire accurately enables people to choose between functions when they answer the questions. Similarly, research is routinely updated by CPP Inc to demonstrate that the test is consistent (reliable) and that it measures what it claims to measure (valid).

There are quite a few critics of the MBTI who argue that neither the Myers–Briggs nor the Jungian models offer any scientific, experimental proof to support the existence of or interrelationship between the functions. Boyle (1995), for example, says that there are serious limitations in MBTI reliability and validity, arguing that its routine use in organizational and occupational settings is not recommended. Pittenger (2005) suggests that while it may be very popular, 'considerable caution' is warranted when drawing conclusions from the four-letter formula.

In spite of criticism from research psychologists and others, MBTI is perceived as intuitively helpful and it remains the psychometric tool of choice for many professionals.

Leadership challenge

Ask your team to complete the MBTI (using a licensed facilitator). Work with your team to understand differences and similarities in ways of working.

More help

Key reference

Myers, I B (2003) *MBTI Manual: A guide to the development and use of the Myers–Briggs type indicator*, CPP, Mountain View, CA

Other references

Boyle, G J (1995) Myers–Briggs type indicator (MBTI): some psychometric limitations, *Australian Psychologist*, 30 (1), pp 71–4

Jung, C G (1923) *Psychological Types: Or the psychology of individuation*, Harcourt, Brace, New York

Myers, I B (1962) *The Myers–Briggs Type Indicator*, Consulting Psychologists Press, Palo Alto, CA

Myers, I B and Myers, P B (1995) *Gifts Differing: Understanding personality type*, Davies-Black Publishing, Palo Alto, CA

Pittenger, D J (2005) Cautionary comments regarding the Myers–Briggs type indicator, *Consulting Psychology Journal: Practice and Research*, 57 (3), pp 210–21

How do we know if someone is telling us a lie?
Facial displays

14

The big idea

Paul Ekman pioneered the study of the connection between people's emotions and their facial expressions. His initial work focused on understanding non-verbal communication in relationships (Ekman and Friesen, 1969). In the early 1970s he studied tribespeople in Papua New Guinea and found that facial expressions in response to an emotion such as anger are universal and not simply determined by culture (Ekman and Friesen, 1971). He discovered that expressions of shame, joy, disgust, anger, sadness and surprise are well recognized regardless of a person's background. Building on this research, Ekman developed the Facial Action Coding System or FACS (Ekman and Friesen, 1978). This system enables trained coders to categorize every possible facial movement according to the muscles, or action units, involved in the expression. Training to do this is available through Ekman's own company. More recently he has developed training materials to help people to recognize signs of emotion in the face (Facial Expression. Awareness. Compassion. Emotions. or F.A.C.E). Tools which support this include the Micro-Expression training package. This trains people to notice expressions of concealed emotion. Another tool enables people to recognize subtle expressions of emotion that otherwise may be missed. Both of these are available to download for a fee via the internet (Paul Ekman Training, 2011).

Ekman is particularly well known for his work on what has become known as The Wizards Project (Ekman and O'Sullivan, 1991). This research appears to show that relatively few people can, by noticing facial expressions, naturally spot when someone is lying. Only 50 'Truth Wizards' were identified out of the 20,000 people who took part. The claim is that, with a short amount of training, people can improve their ability to spot when they are being told a lie by noticing micro-expressions that give the game away.

So what?

FACS has been used to help train a wide range of professionals, from psychologists through to cartoon animators. The detail in the FACS manual is now viewed as the world-standard coding tool for facial expressions. The Wizards Project is much better known to the general public and has been used as the basis for the very popular US drama series *Lie to Me*. It has also had significant media exposure and associated bestselling books. The training to identify concealed expressions is, unsurprisingly, particularly popular with crime detection agencies who, with the exception of the US Secret Service, came out as no better at identifying them than any other group. Ekman's work has been applied to airport security processes and he is currently developing computer facial recognition software to extend the use of his system.

Ekman and his colleagues recognize that the reasons people lie in social situations can be quite complex and not necessarily amenable to clear interpretation. Facial expressions and the general demeanour of a person can only point to the need to ask further questions rather than jumping to conclusions that they have lied. They are keen to emphasize that they have not developed a lie detection system: 'Most of us would do well to entertain some skepticism about our ability to detect deception form demeanour' (Ekman and O'Sullivan, 1991).

What else?

Ekman's ideas have their critics. Bond *et al*, for example, say that the identification of Truth Wizards was no more than an expected statistical occurrence and does not prove anything about who may or may may not possess lie detection abilities (Bond and Uysal, 2007). Others have suggested that the research itself used mainly artificial situations which skewed the findings (Vrij, 2004). The use of Ekman's ideas in the 'Screening Passengers by Observation Techniques' (SPOT) programme in the United States has come under criticism for not being subject to proper scientific testing. Recent high-profile cases where passengers have been wrongly assessed as presenting a security threat have added to the questions being asked about the reliability of the system.

Ekman has not subjected recent research for peer review, arguing that this will present national security issues for the United States. As a result, his colleagues feel that they are not properly able to test his findings.

Leadership challenge

Visit Paul Ekman's website (**http://www.paulekman.com/**) and try out some of the sample training sessions. What is the relevance to your own leadership?

More help

Key references

Ekman, P and Friesen, W V (1978) *Facial Action Coding System: A technique for the measurement of facial movement*, Consulting Psychologists Press, Palo Alto, CA

Ekman, P and O'Sullivan, M (1991) Who can catch a liar? *American Psychologist*, **46** (9), pp 913–20

Other references

Bond, C F and Uysal, A (2007) On lie detection 'wizards', *Law and Human Behavior*, **31** (1), pp 109–15

Ekman, P and Friesen, W V (1969) The repertoire of nonverbal behavior: categories, origins, usage, and coding, *Semiotica*, **1** (1), pp 49–98

Ekman, P and Friesen, W V (1971) Constants across cultures in the face and emotion, *Journal of Personality and Social Psychology*, **17** (2), pp 124–9

Paul Ekman training [accessed 15 September 2011] www.ekmaninternational.com

Vrij, A (2004) Why professionals fail to catch liars and how they can improve, *Legal and Criminological Psychology*, **9** (2), pp 159–81

15

How can people understand and build on their strengths?

Values in Action Inventory of Strengths (VIA-IS)

The big idea

Until the advent of positive psychology in the late 1990s, the majority of psychology was concerned with understanding how problems or illnesses can be 'cured'. This focus is owed, in part, to the role psychology has historically played in helping people cope with the trauma caused by war. It also has to do with the aspiration of psychology to develop as a scientific discipline by using approaches and statistical techniques that resolve known problems.

An example of this problem-focused approach is found in clinical psychology where psychiatrists and psychologists use a common set of definitions to describe people's illnesses. This is the *Diagnostic and Statistical Manual* or DSM (American Psychiatric Association, Task Force on DSM-IV, 2000).

Professor Martin Seligman turned this approach on its head, arguing, among other things, that people grow in the direction of their strengths, and thus we should focus on these rather than concentrating on weaknesses. He argued that such an approach can help people become healthier, more fulfilled, confident and focused. In short, it's not the absence of psychological problems that matters most but rather the development and maintenance of psychological health.

To help shift the focus onto psychological health, Seligman and his colleague Professor Christopher Peterson compiled a *Character and Strengths Handbook* which classifies positive human strengths (Peterson and Seligman, 2004). This classification is based on several assumptions: first, that human strengths are not secondary to weaknesses; second, that they can be understood scientifically; and finally, that they differentiate people, are similar to traits but can be influenced by the environment. The process of compiling the handbook involved wide-ranging literature reviews and extensive consultation with academics and psychologists. To narrow down the initial list of strengths, they applied criteria which were intended to ensure that strengths included in the list are measurable, demonstrable in people's behaviours and contribute to a fulfilled life. The final result is 24 character strengths organized into six virtues (Table 15.1).

TABLE 15.1   Twenty-four character strengths organized into six virtues

Virtue	Indicative strengths
Wisdom and knowledge	Creativity Curiosity Judgement, open-mindedness Love of learning Perspective, wisdom
Courage	Bravery Perseverance, industriousness Honesty, authenticity, integrity Zest and enthusiasm
Love and humanity	Capacity to love and be loved Kindness and generosity Social intelligence
Justice	Teamwork Fairness Leadership
Temperance	Self-control Forgiveness and mercy Modesty and humility Prudence
Transcendence	Appreciation of beauty and excellence Gratitude Hope, optimism, future-mindedness Humour Spirituality

SOURCE: adapted from Peterson and Seligman (2004)

So what?

To make the *Handbook* practically helpful, Peterson and Seligman designed the Values in Action Inventory of Strengths (VIA-IS). This is an assessment tool designed to identify a person's profile of character strengths. The basic report is available free to anyone on the internet and it takes between 30 and 40 minutes to complete the 240 questions: **https://www.viame.org/**.

Assuming that proponents of positive psychology are correct when they say that top achievers put effort into building on their strengths rather than resolving their weaknesses, the VIA-IS has great potential in a work context to support individual development (Clifton and Anderson, 2002). For example, an employer may ask all staff to complete the survey and then discuss with them how they could develop their strengths in the context of the workplace. Alternatively, a company may choose to develop a coaching culture among its managers. Such a culture could be specifically orientated towards developing the strengths in people rather than taking a more traditional problem-solving approach.

Boniwell highlights a number of questions about using the strengths approach, including the concern, echoed by others, that the classification of strengths is perhaps neither as comprehensive nor as measurable as initially claimed. The use of self-report questionnaires may not be an accurate measure of strengths and could just reflect personal perception rather than actual strengths evidenced in behaviour. Maybe a person knowing their weaknesses and seeking to improve them are not a bad thing in itself. When taken with the potential danger of people overdeveloping their strengths there is an argument for a balance between working with strengths and weaknesses at a personal level (Boniwell, 2006).

What else?

It is worth noting that the validity and reliability of the VIA-IS continue to be the subject of debate and ongoing research (Park, Peterson and Seligman, 2004). There are also different perspectives on the categorization of strengths (Shryack *et al*, 2010). One question people ask is whether or not the strengths in the *Handbook* reflect US culture or are reflected in the values and behaviours of other nations. Research by Park *et al* suggests that the strengths in VIA-IS are broadly universally recognized (Park, Peterson and Seligman, 2006).

An alternative approach has focused on the deployment of strengths and has been developed into an assessment tool – Gallup's StrengthsFinder. This online test is accessible by first purchasing one of their publications (Rath, 2007). This tool focuses on talents rather than strengths. Clifton and Anderson suggest that a talent is the capacity to do something. Strengths become evident when a talent has been developed through the application of knowledge and skills (Clifton and Anderson, 2002).

Leadership challenge

Take the free VIA-IS test. Reflect on your results. How might you better play to your own strengths in leading your team?

More help

For the VIA-IS assessment test: **https://www.viame.org/**

Key reference

Peterson, C and Seligman, M E P (2004) *Character Strengths and Virtues: A handbook and classification*, Oxford University Press, New York

Other references

American Psychiatric Association, Task Force on DSM-IV (2000) *Diagnostic and Statistical Manual of Mental Disorders: DSM-IV-TR*, American Psychiatric Publishing, Inc, Arlington, VA

Boniwell, I (2006) *Positive Psychology in a Nutshell: A balanced introduction to the science of optimal functioning*, Personal Well-Being Centre, London

Clifton, D O and Anderson, E (2002) *StrengthsQuest*, The Gallup Organization, Princeton, NJ

Park, N, Peterson, C and Seligman, M E P (2004) Strengths of character and well-being, *Journal of Social and Clinical Psychology*, **23** (5), pp 603–19

Park, N, Peterson, C and Seligman, M E P (2006) Character strengths in fifty-four nations and the fifty US states, *Journal of Positive Psychology*, **1** (3), pp 118–29

Rath, T (2007) *StrengthsFinder 2.0: A new and upgraded edition of the online test from Gallup's Now Discover Your Strengths*, Gallup Press, New York

Shryack, J, Steger, M F, Krueger, R F *et al* (2010) The structure of virtue: an empirical investigation of the dimensionality of the virtues in action inventory of strengths, *Personality and Individual Differences*, **48** (6), pp 714–19

16

What can employers do to improve the mood and commitment of their staff?

Psychological capital

The big idea

Psychological capital (PsyCap) is defined by its originator, Professor Fred Luthans as:

> An individual's positive psychological state of development that is characterized by:
>
> 1 Having confidence (self-efficacy) to take on and put in the necessary effort to succeed at a challenging task.
> 2 Making a positive attribution (optimism) about succeeding now and in the future.
> 3 Persevering toward goals and, when necessary, redirecting paths to goals (hope) in order to succeed.
> 4 When beset by problems and adversity, sustaining and bouncing back and even beyond (resilience) to attain success.
>
> (Luthans, Youssef and Avolio, 2007a)

Psychological capital emphasizes human development and performance improvement. Luthans and his colleagues focus on psychological 'states' rather than personality traits. A state is a mood or feeling. These are transient human phenomena which come and go, and consequently have the potential to be induced or developed. Personality traits, on the other hand, are considered fairly fixed and less amenable to change (Lewis, 2011).

Psychological capital incorporates four specific psychological states that can be developed, are amenable to measurement, relevant to the workplace and life enhancing. The first is self-efficacy, a person's self-belief in their ability to perform a particular task. Hope, including willpower, is the second. The third is optimism and the fourth resilience. Research to date indicates that the combination of all four states is a better predictor of performance in the workplace than if you consider the effect of each of the individual components on their own (Luthans *et al*, 2010).

So what?

To establish the impact of psychological capital on workplace performance, Luthans and his colleagues developed an online survey tool, the Psychological Capital Questionnaire (PCQ). Using this and other research methodologies, they found that people who demonstrate high levels of psychological capital:

- Express lower levels of workplace cynicism because of their generally positive emotions and the belief that their effort will make a difference.
- Are less likely to want to change job as frequently as those with a low level of psychological capital. Their outlook is that they can cope with any challenge and prefer to persevere rather than simply swap jobs.
- Have lower rates of absenteeism and are likely to encourage other workers in supporting the achievement of organizational goals.
- Respond better to stressful events and do not experience negative repercussions as powerfully.
- Generally perform better in their jobs.

(Avey, Luthans and Youssef, 2010)

There is also evidence that having employees with high levels of psychological capital will enable organizational change to proceed much more smoothly than otherwise would be the case. Positive emotions help workers to broaden their point of view, encourage openness and honesty in decision making and sustain enthusiasm through the change process (Avey, Wernsing and Luthans, 2008).

So how can employers create in their organizations the conditions that encourage the development of psychological capital in their staff? Self-efficacy can be developed by giving staff opportunities to excel at new tasks, providing good role models, encouraging people to express confidence in their abilities and ensuring that people care for their own well-being. Hope can be encouraged by involving staff in personal goal-setting processes, team planning, decision making and reinforcing hopeful behaviours. Encouraging self-forgiveness and helping staff to spot new opportunities will help develop optimism. And finally, resilience will grow if people learn from their experiences and become more aware of how their moods affect them during stressful times.

Practically, Luthans and colleagues suggest short two–three-hour work-shops on psychological capital as 'micro interventions'. They find that these micro sessions have a significant developmental impact on staff and the wider organization, resulting in performance gains (Luthans *et al*, 2007a).

What else?

Researchers acknowledge that it is not always possible to say that one action directly causes an increase in psychological capital. There is also a range of other factors that impact on people's moods and self-confidence. The organizational climate is one such factor. It can have a significant bearing on psychological capital and has not been subject to as much research (Luthans *et al*, 2007b). There is further work to be done on establishing the relevance of psychological capital to non-US cultures and to determine if further constructs should be added to it to make it a more comprehensive measure (Avey *et al*, 2010; Luthans *et al*, 2005).

Leadership challenge

Think about the four components of 'psychological capital'. How might you use each one of these to increase the commitment of members of your team?

More help

Key reference

Luthans, F, Youssef, C M and Avolio, B J (2007a) *Psychological Capital: Developing the human competitive edge*, Oxford University Press, New York

Other references

Avey, J B, Luthans, F, Smith, R M and Palmer, N F (2010) Impact of positive psychological capital on employee well-being over time, *Journal of Occupational Health Psychology*, **15** (1), pp 17–28

Avey, J B, Luthans, F and Youssef, C M (2010) The additive value of positive psychological capital in predicting work attitudes and behaviors, *Journal of Management*, **36** (2), pp 430–52

Avey, J B, Wernsing, T S and Luthans, F (2008) Can positive employees help positive organizational change? Impact of psychological capital and emotions on relevant attitudes and behaviors, *Journal of Applied Behavioral Science*, **44** (1), pp 48–70

Lewis, S (2011) *Positive Psychology at Work*, 1st edn, Wiley-Blackwell, Oxford

Luthans, F, Avey, J B, Avolio, B J *et al* (2010) The development and resulting perform-ance impact of positive psychological capital, *Human Resource Development Quarterly*, **21** (1), pp 41–67

Luthans, F, Avolio, B J, Avey, J B *et al* (2007b) Positive psychological capital: measure-ment and relationship with performance and satisfaction, *Personnel Psychology*, **60** (3), pp 541–72

Luthans, F, Avolio, B J, Walumbwa, F O *et al* (2005) The psychological capital of Chinese workers: exploring the relationship with performance, *Management and Organization Review*, **1** (2), pp 249–71

17

How to help people cope well with change

Three phases of transition

The big idea

William Bridges, a management consultant and author, is most well known for the idea that when managing change in organizations it's important to differentiate between 'change' and 'transition'. He argues that change is the actual circumstance, like a new factory, new boss, new policy or new job. Transition, on the other hand, is the psychological, or inner, process through which people come to terms with change (Bridges, 2009). His idea has become very popular and while it has not been subject to rigorous academic testing, many change leaders speak of it making intuitive sense (Mackinnon, 2007).

Bridges's theory has three phases:

1 Ending, Losing, Letting Go – helping people deal with their tangible and intangible losses and prepare to move on.

2 The Neutral Zone – this is where critical psychological changes take place and can involve confusion and disorientation.

3 The New Beginning – helping people to develop a new identity and sense of purpose which enables them to make the change work.

(Bridges, 2003)

His argument is that what often makes change difficult for people is not the practicalities, nor even the rationale for it, but rather their own internal psychological turmoil. For change to be managed well, this human aspect of change also needs careful attention.

The theory is often presented as a diagram (Figure 17.1).

The X or horizontal axis represents time and the Y or vertical axis managerial activity. So, at the start of a transition, managerial focus needs to be on helping people let go of the past. Later, the focus shifts to investing in the future. The Neutral Zone in between is the psychological 'space' where

FIGURE 17.1   Bridges's three phases of transition

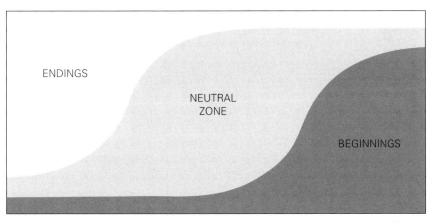

ENDINGS

NEUTRAL
ZONE

BEGINNINGS

Past   **Future**

SOURCE: adapted from Bridges (2003)

people sense they are between two places, perhaps standing still or perhaps experiencing turmoil. It is a place of both risk and opportunity. People may find themselves drawn back to old familiar ways of thinking as they become anxious about what the future holds. Alternatively, they may become excited about future possibilities that they begin to see on the horizon. Bridges suggests that this is where managers need to give people particular support. The opportunity is there for people also to identify and find new ways of doing things. Managers can capitalize on this if they are aware of it.

The diagram is helpful because it also emphasizes the point that endings, neutrality and beginnings can be happening at the same time for an individual. All three states can be in play and, of course, how this manifests itself will differ between individuals.

Bridges differentiates between 'starts' and 'beginnings'. A beginning occurs when people have adopted new understandings, attitudes and values, while a start takes place at a designated point on the schedule as a result of rational decisions. Again, this reinforces the point that transition is not to be confused with change.

So what?

To give focus at the start of a change process, Bridges recommends that leaders use the following questions to begin planning a transition:

1 Describe the change in as much detail as you can.

2 Identify the secondary changes that the change will probably
cause – and the further changes that those changes will cause.

3 Determine how people will be affected – who will have to let go of something?

4 Think of this from the subjective viewpoint of people affected.

5 Beyond these losses, is there something that is over for everyone?

There are plenty of other practical ideas that Bridges offers to help managers support staff through transition. The principal ones are shown in Table 17.1.

TABLE 17.1 Practical ideas to help managers support staff through transition

Stage	Tools
1. Ending, Losing, Letting Go	• Assess transition readiness by using a staff survey. • Develop a transition plan. • Establish a transition monitoring team. • Constantly communicate the benefits of the new state. • Implement training and staff development programmes that help people manage transitions for themselves and their staff. • Ensure that leaders are available for staff meetings to provide updates and reassurance. • Build a shared vision of the future with staff.
2. The Neutral Zone	• Publish the implementation plan for the whole process. • Provide opportunities for staff to have one-to-one meetings with key leaders. • Review progress and possibly take another survey of staff attitudes. • Provide development opportunities and career advice. • Offer support for people as they take on new roles. • Encourage managers to demonstrate empathy and active listening to staff concerns. • Anticipate ebbs and flows in levels of engagement.
3. The New Beginning	• Use storytelling to help people reflect on their experiences and move forward. • Ensure that people have the opportunity to meet with managers for one-to-one conversations. • Avoid blaming people for mistakes they make in the new situation.

SOURCE: adapted from Bridges (2003)

What else?

Many people appear to find the model useful as a prompt rather than as a step-by-step change plan, which is something Bridges never intended it to be in the first place (Allison, 2002; Bridges, 1991; Goodman, Schlossberg and Anderson, 2006; Speck, 1996). There also appears to be no formal psychological evaluation of the model. Some criticism is levelled at Bridges for some of the complexity of the language and a resulting lack of clarity in distinguishing between change and transition. Critics argue that real-life change is much more complicated than the model. Furthermore, Bridges concentrates on individual impacts of change rather than considering the social and cultural aspects of a change process (Mackinnon, 2007).

Leadership challenge

Reflect on a personal transition you are experiencing currently. How does Bridges's model help you? Test out the model on a change process you are engaged with in an organization. What are the benefits and what does not work so well?

More help

Key reference

Bridges, W (2009) *Managing Transitions: Making the most of change*, Da Capo Lifelong Books, Cambridge, MA

Other references

Allison, M (2002) Into the fire: boards and executive transitions, *Nonprofit Management and Leadership*, **12** (4), pp 341–51
Bridges, W (1991) *Managing Transitions*, Perseus Publishing, Cambridge, MA
Bridges, W (2003) *Managing Transitions*, Da Capo Press, Cambridge, MA
Goodman, J, Schlossberg, N K and Anderson, M L (2006) *Counseling Adults in Transition: Linking practice with theory*, Springer, New York
Mackinnon, L (2007 [accessed 22 October 2011]) *Managing Transitions Book Review* [Online] http://www.think-differently.org/2007/05/book-review-managing-transitions-by/
Speck, M (1996) The change process in a school learning community, *School Community Journal*, **6**, pp 69–80

18 Where does motivation come from? Self-determination theory

The big idea

Self-determination theory (SDT) is a meta-theory developed over the past 30 years by two psychology professors, Richard Ryan and Edward Deci. This family of theories is concerned with motivation and personality. The focus is on understanding the interplay between those things that motivate a person from outside themselves, extrinsic motivators such as pay and recognition, and intrinsic motivators such as values, curiosity, creativity and personal commitment.

Self-determination theory itself belongs to a wider family of positive psychology theories which focus on understanding how to fulfil the potential for human growth and well-being. In this context Ryan and Deci take an organismic perspective on human development. They believe that people are actively engaged in mastering the challenges life presents them and then using all of their experiences to build a coherent identity. This integrating process happens when the surrounding environment supports it.

Through their research Ryan and Deci conclude that a person's sense of well-being, and consequently motivation to grow, is likely to be heightened when three fundamental human needs are met. These are: first, autonomy, the need to be able to choose what they do; second, having a sense of competence, a belief that they know what they are doing; and third, relatedness, the ability to participate in human relationships that are fulfilling and secure. To access these psychological 'nutriments', Ryan and Deci suggest that people need to live in environments that are supportive and motivational in the broadest sense. Where such external support is absent, people's experience of life and work is not as fulfilling as it might otherwise be.

Self-determination theory contains at least five 'mini-theories', each emerging out of research aimed at determining the nature of the extrinsic and intrinsic motivation:

1 Cognitive evaluation theory (CET) concerns intrinsic motivations and how they may be impacted by external factors.

2 Organismic integration theory (OIT) looks at extrinsic motivations and how they can become internalized.

3 Causality orientations theory (COT) considers the role played in motivation by individual differences.

4 Basic psychological needs theory (BPNT) explores the roles played by competence, autonomy and relatedness in well-being.

5 Goal contents theory (GCT) reviews the different types of goals associated with extrinsic and intrinsic motivation.

During the past decade the scope of self-determination theory has continued to expand, and it now incorporates research and theory related to aspects of vitality, mindfulness, the experience of nature and contingent self-esteem. Overviews of the theory can be found in a wide range of published articles. Some of the key ones are referenced at the end of the chapter. Further background articles are also available from the home website of Professors Ryan and Deci at the University of Rochester (**http://www.psych.rochester.edu/SDT/**).

So what?

The theory has been applied in practice to many aspects of life, including education, physical health, mental well-being and sports. The literature referenced below also contains a number of practical applications to organizational life and work, including:

- *Feedback*. Providing expected and unexpected positive feedback can enhance a person's sense of competence, as can ensuring that work tasks offer the optimal level of challenge.

- *Rewards*. Providing rewards such as pay bonuses which are contingent on performance can undermine intrinsic motivation. This may go some way to explaining why managers can be perplexed when they assume that a reward package will enhance performance when in reality its effect is either neutral or even negative.

- *Productivity*. Ensuring positive relationships between employees will enhance relatedness and productivity.

- *Autonomy of decision making*. Enabling people to make decisions about how they do their work meets a psychological need for autonomy and is likely to encourage attitudes and behaviours that demonstrate higher levels of motivation. There is also some evidence that it will reduce emotional burnout.

- *Internalizing of extrinsic motivations*. It's possible for work behaviours that were originally stimulated by extrinsic factors, such as payment by results, to ultimately become owned by individuals and assimilated into people's own set of values and personal motivation. Over time, the behaviour becomes part of the employee's self-concept.

- *Motivating staff doing boring tasks*. Managers can motivate staff by helping them connect boring tasks with core values, acknowledging their feelings, providing information and offering some choice when possible.

- *Exposing staff to natural environments*. There is some evidence that exposing staff to nature can enhance a sense of autonomy. This in turn builds intrinsic motivation.

- *Creativity*. High levels of intrinsic motivation, supported by a positive work environment, will encourage creativity. The slight cautionary note is that the creative ideas themselves might not have direct practical application to the job. Nonetheless, feeling creative at work will build a positive sense of competence and autonomy in the employee.

- *The attractiveness of self-employment/temporary work*. For some people, working as self-employed and/or on short-term contracts enhances their sense of autonomy, competence and overall self-determination. This then results in high levels of intrinsic motivation. Employers should consider the types of contracts they offer staff, with a view to building both intrinsic and extrinsic motivation.

What else?

Given its breadth, it is unsurprising that the theory has its critics, for example Locke and Latham (1990) who dispute the concept as a whole and comment that if rewards prove detrimental to motivating staff, the theory has no practical relevance. It is an expanding area of research and many of the constructs emerging from the theory are only beginning to be explored by others.

Leadership challenge

Compare the practical applications of this theory with your own organization's management and employment practices. Are there changes you can make, or influence others to make, that will build both intrinsic and extrinsic motivation in your workforce?

Reflect on what steps you could take to grow your own motivation as a leader.

More help

The University of Rochester self-determination theory website: **http://www.psych.rochester.edu/SDT/**

Key reference

Deci, E L and Ryan, R M (1985) *Intrinsic Motivation and Self-Determination in Human Behavior*, Springer, New York

Other references

Deci, E L, Connell, J P and Ryan, R M (1989) Self-determination in a work organization, *Journal of Applied Psychology*, **74** (4), pp 580–90

Deci, E L, Koestner, R and Ryan, R M (1999) A meta-analytic review of experiments examining the effects of extrinsic rewards on intrinsic motivation, *Psychological Bulletin*, **125** (6), pp 627–68

Deci, E L, and Ryan, R M (2000) The 'what' and 'why' of goal pursuits: human needs and the self-determination of behavior, *Psychological Inquiry*, **11** (4), pp 227–68

Locke, E A and Latham, G P (1990) *A Theory of Goal Setting and Task Performance*, Prentice-Hall, Englewood Cliffs, NJ

Ryan, R M and Deci, E L (2000) Self-determination theory and the facilitation of intrinsic motivation, social development, and well-being, *American Psychologist*, **55** (1), pp 68–78

Ryan, R M and Deci, E L (2001) On happiness and human potentials: a review of research on hedonic and eudaimonic well-being, *Annual Review of Psychology*, **52** (1), pp 141–66

How can we rely on psychometric tests?

Reliability and validity

The big idea

Psychometrics are a broad range of assessments and measurements designed to test intelligence, skills, aptitude, educational achievement and personality traits. When a test claims to measure one or more of these, in classic test theory it has to demonstrate reliability and validity. A reliable measure is one that will provide the same result (score) over time. It is dependable. A valid measure is one that measures what it claims to measure. These definitions are straightforward enough but because business psychology, and psychology generally, deals with things that cannot easily be observed from the outside, such as how someone feels about an issue, ensuring reliability and validity can be difficult. It is, of course, possible for a measure to be reliable without being valid. It may be good at measuring something but what it is measuring is not what you need it to measure!

Reliability

Reliability can be assessed statistically. One way of doing this is the Pearson Correlation Coefficient or test–retest reliability. Participants take the same test twice with a time lag between each completion of the test. If the test produces a similar (or the same) score on each occasion, the test has high reliability. To rely on the result of this test it's important to make sure that conditions when the two tests take place are as similar as possible. Another option, though more costly, is developing parallel forms. In this test developers produce two sets of similiar tests, each tested for reliability, which they then evaluate against each another. Both these approaches are *external* forms of reliability. *Internal* reliability checks how different parts of the same measure produce results which match with one another. Statistical tests for this include Cronbach's coefficient alpha and the 'split-half' test which is achieved through correlating two halves of a test. The result is then adjusted using the Spearman–Brown prediction formula.

Validity

Validity is finding out if what you want to discover about someone is actually being measured by the test you are using. Criterion-related validity uses a list of expected participant behaviours, some of which may be objective, such as the number of items produced, or subjective, such as the view of a supervisor. It can be a combination of both. A comparison is then made with actual participant test scores. If the participant's predicted performance matches the test scores, criterion-related validity is high. If the participant performs poorly in the actual task but the test suggested that they should do well, validity is low. Statistically this is presented as a validity coefficient.

There are several ways of calculating a validity coefficient, some more complex than others. Once it has been calculated, it is best practice to cross-check the results on a second sample of participants to cross-validate the findings.

Other types of validation are often used. If a test looks and feels right it is said to have 'face validity'. If a company is convinced by the sales pitch that the test is a good one to use with their employees, it has 'faith' validity! Content validity ensures that the technical or practical activities involved in a job are included in the test. Construct validity is more complex and involves taking psychological characteristics such as emotional intelligence and linking them to events or activities which may be observable and so also measurable. These links are then tested to ensure that the test and the construct fit with one another.

So what?

Psychometric tests are used extensively in recruitment, promotion and management development. They are also sometimes used in performance appraisal. All of these are vital functions for a company to get right. Whether tests are reliable and valid is thus an important consideration for those involved in selection and development in choosing which tests to use.

Organizations have increasingly become aware that fairness is important for employees and, if the employment relationship breaks down, may be challenged in a court of law. Demonstrably adhering to anti-discriminatory selection and employment legislation is important reputationally and financially. Picking valid and reliable tests will undoubtedly help an organization defend itself against unfairness claims.

Looking at a range of studies, Arnold and Randall (2010) conclude that the highest levels of evidence for criterion-related validity in selection methods can be found in structured interviews, cognitive ability tests, situational judgement tests and work sample tests. Personality measures come out as moderate and, unsurprisingly, employer references low. Assessment centres which use a combination of these methods come out as high on the criterion-validity scale and thus are arguably the most effective when seeking to select new staff or make choices about which staff to develop.

What else?

Alongside reliability and validity there are other factors that must be taken into account when using particular tests. These include legality, practicality in administering them, applicant reactions and the usefulness of the information for feedback purposes. It is also important to ensure that tests are administered by trained individuals and that the process of testing maintains the integrity of a test.

Organizations and professional associations increasingly look at the measures, not just with regard to a job role, but also with relevance to the wider business and social environment. Companies that develop and sell psychometric tests need to balance the economics of ensuring the highest levels of reliability with the fees customers are prepared to pay. There is usually an ongoing investment needed to update tests to meet changing circumstances.

Technically there are challenges in ensuring validity and reliability. Arnold and Randall (2010) highlight sampling error, poor measurement precision and a restricted range of scores potentially affecting validity. The best test publishers provide background information on validity and reliability, as well as norm groups (which people were used in the research). Before selecting tests organizations should clearly understand the data supporting the test they are proposing to use and whether the test is appropriate for the group they are going to test.

Leadership challenge

What experience have you had of using tests (either setting them or completing them)? Were you aware of the validity and reliability scores of the test you were taking/setting? How will you select tests in the future?

More help

Key references

Arnold, J and Randall, R (2010) *Work Psychology: Understanding human behaviour in the workplace*, 5th edn, Pearson Education, Harlow

McKenna, E F (2006) *Business Psychology and Organizational Behaviour*, 4th edn, Psychology Press, Hove, Sussex

Other references

Cronbach, L J and Gleser, G C (1965) *Psychological Tests and Personnel Decisions*, University of Illinois Press, Champaign

Hunsley, J and Meyer, G J (2003) The incremental validity of psychological testing and assessment: conceptual, methodological, and statistical issues, *Psychological Assessment*, **15** (4), pp 446–55

Meyer, G J, Finn, S E, Eyde, L D *et al* (2001) Psychological testing and psychological assessment: a review of evidence and issues, *American Psychologist*, **56** (2), pp 128–65

Passmore, J (2009) *Psychometrics in Coaching*, Kogan Page, London

20 How can people change their behaviours?
Transtheoretical Model of Change

The big idea

Professor of psychology James Prochaska is a researcher in cancer prevention and originator of this theory of behaviour change. He combines a wide range of theories into one model, hence the title, *Transtheoretical* Model of Change (TTM). It is sometimes called the Stages of Change model (SoC). Since he first published his ideas in the early 1980s the model has been refined but the basic premise remains the same. It is intended to be a comprehensive model of the stages through which a person goes as they change their behaviour. The core of the model is five stages of change (Figure 20.1).

FIGURE 20.1 Transtheoretical Model of Change

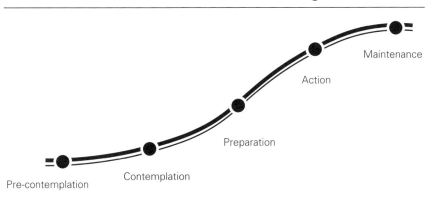

Maintenance

Action

Preparation

Contemplation

Pre-contemplation

SOURCE: adapted from Prochaska and DiClemente (1982)

1 Pre-contemplation. Individuals at this stage are not really thinking about changing behaviour. They are not aware of the impact of their behaviour, upon either themselves or others. They are likely to be unmotivated.

2 Contemplation. People at this point have become aware of a need to change their behaviour. They are considering whether or not they should take steps to change. They are usually quite ambivalent about their situation and therefore feel quite 'stuck'.

3 Preparation. At this stage people have largely resolved their uncertainty and decided that they should plan to take action. It may be, however, that they are still not 100% committed to a change plan.

4 Action. People at this point are already halfway through the behaviour change process. It is also the point at which people may return to the first stage if they have not fully prepared their plan of action.

5 Maintenance. Individuals are considered to be at this stage if they have successfully maintained the new behaviour for a period of at least six months.

(Prochaska, Johnson and Lee, 1998)

The model proposes that people move through the stages of change over a period of time. It does not quantify the actual length of time people will spend in each stage, accepting that individuals will move through at their own pace. The model is often presented diagrammatically as a spiral or staircase, acknowledging the reality that people will often move backwards and forwards between the stages.

Underpinning the five stages are three approaches to measuring change. The first is the idea that people will always weigh up the pros and cons of changing and is taken from the decisional balance construct (Janis and Mann, 1977). The second is from the idea of self-efficacy, or self-confidence, originally developed by Albert Bandura (Bandura, 1977); and the third is the notion of target behaviour (Prochaska *et al*, 1998). There are questionnaires available to help measure each of these.

So what?

Prochaska and his colleagues identify 10 distinct processes that enable change to happen across all five stages. The first set of five are experiential processes and are most useful in the early stages (Table 20.1).

The second set are behavioural processes and are most useful in the later stages (Table 20.2).

The main application of this model tends to be related to health promotion and well-being. There are many references to its usefulness to smoking cessation strategies, managing obesity and alcoholism recovery. The model

TABLE 20.1   Experiential processes

Process of change	Actions
1. Consciousness raising	Provide information about the consequences of not changing behaviour and the benefits of changing.
2. Dramatic relief	Offer personal stories about people who have changed, and use role-play to highlight what changed behaviour could look and feel like.
3. Environmental re-evaluation	Help the person understand the impact of their current behaviour on others and the wider environment.
4. Social liberation	Provide social opportunities that encourage changes in behaviour.
5. Self re-evaluation	Encourage the person to see themselves from new perspectives.

SOURCE: adapted from Prochaska and DiClemente (1983)

TABLE 20.2   Behavioural processes

Process of change	Actions
1. Stimulus control	Prompt change of behaviour by removing things that trigger old behaviours and putting in place positive encouragements.
2. Helping relationship	Enable supportive relationships that encourage perseverance towards achieving the target behaviour.
3. Counter-conditioning	Support the learning of new behaviours that will replace old behaviours.
4. Reinforcement management	Build in reinforcements and rewards for new behaviours.
5. Self-liberation	Encourage people to tell the stories of how they changed and to recommit to continuing the process.

SOURCE: adapted from Prochaska and DiClemente (1983)

has been adopted by motivational interviewing (MI) as its underpinning theory of change (Miller and Rollnick, 2002). MI has been used extensively in counselling behaviour change, such as drug and alcohol addiction, and there is extensive research to support the efficacy of MI as an approach to behaviour change. More recently, writers in business psychology have adapted MI for application in addressing workplace challenges such as dealing with poor performance or employee conflict (Passmore, 2007). Elements of the model can be incorporated into management development programmes to challenge existing behaviours and encourage individuals to think through the stages of change.

What else?

There have been many criticisms of the model from those who work in the field of supporting health-related behaviour change. A randomized trial in 2003, for example, suggested that stage-based interventions are no less effective than non-stage-based approaches (Riemsma *et al*, 2003). There are a number of similar conclusions drawn from research across a range of topics. Some professionals assert that drawing lines between the different stages is unhelpful and not based on evidence. They also argue that the model assumes that people take a coherent and rational approach to deciding to change behaviour. This, they say, is unwarranted given the reality of people's attitudes towards changing behaviour (Brug *et al*, 2005; West, 2005).

Leadership challenge

Are there leadership behaviours that you need to change? Consider how this model might help you make positive changes. How will you know if you have been successful? Are there actions that you can take to help others change their behaviours?

More help

Key reference

Prochaska, J O and DiClemente, C C (1982) Transtheoretical therapy: toward a more integrative model of change, *Psychotherapy: Theory, Research and Practice*, **19** (3), pp 276–88

Other references

Bandura, A (1977) *Social learning theory*, Prentice-Hall, Englewood Cliffs. NJ

Brug, J, Conner, M, Harre, N *et al* (2005) The transtheoretical model and stages of change: a critique, *Health Education Research*, **20** (2), pp 244–58

Janis, I L and Mann, L (1977) *Decision Making: A psychological analysis of conflict, choice, and commitment*, Free Press, New York

Miller, W R and Rollnick, S (2002) *Motivational Interviewing: Preparing people for change*, 2nd edn, Guilford Press, New York

Passmore, J (2007) Addressing deficit performance through coaching: using motivational interviewing for performance improvement in coaching, *International Coaching Psychology Review*, **2** (3), pp 265–79

Prochaska, J O and DiClemente, C C (1983) Stages and processes of self-change of smoking: toward an integrative model of change, *Journal of Consulting and Clinical Psychology*, **51** (3), pp 390–5

Prochaska, J O, Johnson, S and Lee, P (1998) *The Transtheoretical Model of Behavior Change*, Springer, New York

Riemsma, R P, Pattenden, J, Bridle, C *et al* (2003) Systematic review of the effectiveness of stage based interventions to promote smoking cessation, *British Medical Journal*, **326** (7400), pp 1175–7

West, R (2005) Time for a change: putting the transtheoretical (stages of change) model to rest, *Addiction*, **100** (8), pp 1036–9

How do people positively handle trauma?

21

Post-traumatic growth theory

The big idea

The experience of people who have experienced major trauma, perhaps in a car crash or natural disaster, has been the subject of much research over many decades. The reality of post-traumatic stress disorder (PTSD) and its negative health effects are well documented.

A relatively new field of research for psychologists is the idea of 'post-traumatic growth' (PTG). Professor Richard Tedeschi, a psychology professor at the University of North Carolina, coined this phrase to describe the positive personal growth some people experience following their encounter with trauma. Scientific research and the stories of many survivors confirm that not every traumatic experience leads to a persistent negative outlook on life. On the contrary, it can positively help build the capacity of the survivor to face life and grow through it.

There are currently five identified domains of post-traumatic growth:

1 Personal strength. Survivors of trauma speak of becoming personally stronger, resilient, more authentic, open, creative, alive and mature. Many describe themselves as 'better people'.

2 Relating to others. Friendship and family relations seem to get stronger and more meaningful after the trauma. There is a sense of tighter bonds being formed between people.

3 Appreciation for life. People report that after the trauma they value life more profoundly and want to make the most of every day. They also find themselves reflecting more on the meaning of life and their own mortality than they did prior to the event.

4 New possibilities. Survivors often change their life goals and ambitions, perhaps changing career or going to university.

5 Spiritual change. The trauma prompts some people to reconsider their spiritual beliefs and religious practices. There may be a strengthened belief in a higher power.

(Adapted from Hefferon and Boniwell, 2011 and
Tedeschi and Calhoun, 2004)

Reactions to trauma vary between individuals. Researchers have been investigating if there is a link between personality characteristics and post-traumatic growth. Currently there are no definite conclusions. Some studies suggest that people who exhibit extraversion, openness and optimism may be more likely to make the most of the developmental opportunities that trauma may present (Antoni *et al*, 2001). There is also no conclusive evidence about the timing of any growth. Some people seem to report immediate benefits while for others it is years later that any growth is described (Cordova *et al*, 2001).

So what?

There are several different ideas about how post-traumatic growth happens. The shattered-assumptions theory suggests that we all have an inner world where we keep our sense of safety and security. When our sense of security is shattered we then begin a process of rebuilding it, and it is this process that gives us a sense of growth and personal development (Janoff-Bulman, 2002). The organismic valuing theory of growth through adversity assumes that a person must overcome obstacles in their social environment and accommodate new worldviews to obtain any sense of post-traumatic growth (Joseph and Linley, 2008).

The transformational model is the most well known and widely used. It proposes that growth occurs as a result of excessive 'rumination' or cognitive processing. A person who has experienced trauma faces challenges including managing emotional distress, coping with a need to reconsider basic assumptions about life and their life story. To do this they engage in excessive rumination to handle intrusive thoughts, self-disclose to others about what they are experiencing and create a new life narrative. Initially much of this takes place automatically but over time it becomes more deliberate and conscious. It is then that stories of growth through the trauma begin to be told. The model assumes that distress about the trauma coexists with post-traumatic growth (Tedeschi and Calhoun, 1995).

Given the relative newness of the theory, it is unsurprising that there has been almost no research on the relevance of the theory to the workplace. Experience suggests that employees can experience trauma of different types related to employment. These can range from physical assaults or accidents while at work to sudden dismissal and redundancy. An understanding of post-traumatic growth can be helpfully used in these circumstances. When making managerial staff redundant, for example, there may be merit in helping them reflect on what they learned positively from previous traumatic experiences and encouraging them to use this knowledge to access the psychological strength they already possess. This appreciative approach may also stimulate in them some optimism about the future and help them to plan their next steps. The literature also advises that growth cannot be 'pushed' onto someone at times of trauma and that ongoing sensitive mentoring and coaching support is the most appropriate response. Growth is usually recognized some time after the trauma (Hefferon and Boniwell, 2011).

An interesting piece of research has been conducted on ambulance staff who clearly have regular occupational exposure to trauma. The finding of this study is that the vast majority experienced positive post-trauma changes in their lives which they directly attribute to attending work-related traumatic events (Shakespeare-Finch *et al*, 2003).

To assess post-traumatic growth in an individual, a number of web-based questionnaires are available, including the Post Traumatic Growth Inventory (PTGI) (Tedeschi and Calhoun, 1996). This can be accessed free of charge via the link at the end of this chapter.

What else?

There are questions about whether or not post-traumatic growth actually exists. Some psychologists suggest that it may be an illusion or simply a way of rationalizing a very difficult experience. Others argue that it is another form of 'the tyranny of the positive attitude' (Held, 2004). The majority view is that it's a helpful theory and has the potential to provide further useful insights into the effect of trauma on people.

Leadership challenge

Think of a time when you feel you experienced trauma/loss. Try out the Post Traumatic Growth Inventory and reflect on the report. How do you think the trauma has impacted on your view of life and personal leadership style?

More help

To access the Post Traumatic Growth Inventory follow this link:
http://cust-cf.apa.org/ptgi/

Key references

Tedeschi, R G and Calhoun, L G (2004) Posttraumatic growth: conceptual foundations and empirical evidence, *Psychological Inquiry*, **15** (1), pp 1–18

Hefferon, K and Boniwell, I (2011) *Positive Psychology: Theory, research and applications*, Open University Press, Milton Keynes

Other references

Antoni, M, Lehman, J, Kilburn, K *et al* (2001) Cognitive-behavioral stress management intervention decreases the prevalence of depression and enhances the sense of benefit among women under treatment for early-stage breast cancer, *Health Psychology*, **20**, pp 20–32

Cordova, M J, Cunningham, L L C, Carlson, C R *et al* (2001) Posttraumatic growth following breast cancer: a controlled comparison study, *Health Psychology*, **20** (3), pp 176–85

Held, B S (2004) The negative side of positive psychology, *Journal of Humanistic Psychology*, **44** (1), pp 9–46

Janoff-Bulman, R (2002) *Shattered Assumptions*, Free Press, New York

Joseph, S and Linley, P A (2008) *Trauma, Recovery, and Growth: Positive psychological perspectives on posttraumatic stress*, Wiley, Hoboken, NJ

Shakespeare-Finch, J E, Smith, S, Gow, K M *et al* (2003) The prevalence of posttraumatic growth in emergency ambulance personnel, *Traumatology*, **9** (1), pp 58–70

Tedeschi, R G and Calhoun, L G (1995) *Trauma and Transformation: Growing in the aftermath of suffering*, Sage, Thousand Oaks, CA

Tedeschi, R G and Calhoun, L G (1996) The Posttraumatic Growth Inventory: measuring the positive legacy of trauma, *Journal of Traumatic Stress*, **9** (3), pp 455–71

How can people develop their capacity to cope with adversity?
Resilience

22

The big idea

Resilience was first written about extensively in the 1970s and 1980s in relation to the experience of children as they develop into young adults (Garmezy, 1973; Werner and Smith, 1982). It is only with the emergence of positive psychology in the past couple of decades that the adult experience of resilience has been given greater consideration by psychologists. There has been comparatively little research on resilience in the context of the workplace.

Defining resilience has been a challenge for psychologists. One definition is: 'The flexibility in response to changing situational demands, and the ability to bounce back from negative emotional experiences' (Tugade and Fredrickson, 2004).

Lewis builds on this by suggesting that it is not just the 'bouncing back' that is important but the ability to become stronger and more resourceful as a result of the experience (Lewis, 2011). This is related to the concept of post-traumatic growth we considered in Chapter 21.

A slightly more technical but fuller definition of resilience is:

> a dynamic process encompassing positive adaptation within the context of significant adversity. Implicit within this notion are two critical conditions: (1) exposure to significant threat or severe adversity; and (2) the achievement of positive adaptation despite major assaults on the developmental process.
>
> (Luthar, Cicchetti and Becker, 2000: 543)

What this highlights is the view by many that resilience is a process rather than a personality trait and therefore can be learned by individuals. Psychologist Dr Karen Reivich has identified what she calls the seven 'learnable' skills of resilience (Table 22.1).

TABLE 22.1   The seven 'learnable' skills of resilience

Skill	Description
1. Emotion awareness or regulation	Knowing your feelings and, when required, controlling them.
2. Impulse control	Ability to sit back, think carefully about actions and handle ambiguity.
3. Optimism	Realistic optimism about the future.
4. Causal analysis	Taking a comprehensive view of a situation rather than being locked into one particular perspective.
5. Empathy	Connecting well with others, knowing that they can be support for getting through. This reflects a relational dimension of resilience, contrary to the view that it is solely about how an individual reacts from their own inner strength.
6. Self-efficacy	Understanding your strengths and weaknesses, with a confidence to solve problems.
7. Reaching out	Willingness to experience demanding situations in order to grow.

SOURCE: adapted from Reivich and Shatte (2002)

Reivich places optimism as the most important skill to be learned, since this helps people to keep going at times of adversity (Reivich and Shatte, 2002).

Positive psychology expert Sarah Lewis takes a slightly different three-pronged approach. First, she suggests that resilience is achieved as a person builds up resourcefulness and is supported by an organization to do so. This needs to be combined with approaches that help them appreciate the resources they actually have available. Second, encourage people to build up their own risk-reduction strategies in advance of a traumatic event occurring, and third, skill up people to enable them to draw on their knowledge, resourcefulness and risk-reduction strategies at the time they are required (Lewis, 2011).

So what?

Building resilience in employees has clear advantages in demanding contexts and business environments. There are a number of different ideas about how this may be done. Joshua Margolis and Paul Stoltz suggest using a coaching style to ask specifying, visualizing and collaborating questions that challenge people to shift in their thinking across four key resilience domains:

1 Control. A person's response to adversity is governed by the degree to which they believe they have an element of control over it.

2 Impact. A person's belief about their ability to exercise control is affected by their assumptions about what caused the negative event.

3 Breadth. A person is able to respond more effectively to an adverse event if they focus on limiting damage rather than on the wider causes.

4 Duration. Instead of believing that the event will go on for an unlimited period of time, a person is empowered if they can see what future outcomes might emerge at particular points in the future.

A specifying question encourages a concrete response rather than a vague idea. A visualizing question prompts clarity about what a positive future might look like and a collaborating question opens up the person to the idea that other people may help contribute to a successful outcome in the end (Margolis and Stoltz, 2010).

Others have developed a questionnaire to measure resilience (MTQ48) and have offered guidance, based on their models, about how managers may develop stronger resilience (Clough, Earle and Strycharczyk, 2008).

Other ideas to build resilience in employees drawn from a range of sources include:

- training activities that encourage emotional awareness;
- challenging project work and job rotation;
- supporting networking activities and mentoring;
- performance coaching and encouraging the development of a coaching management style across an organization;
- sharing survival stories;
- appropriate use of humour;
- encouraging people to take care of themselves physically and emotionally;
- developing collaborative working across the company.

What else?

Some see resilience as much as a characteristic of an organization as that of the psychological capacity of an individual employee:

As organizations increase their competencies and grow by expanding their behavioural repertoires, they gain possession of a deep and broad range of possible actions they can apply to resolve challenges at hand.

(Sutcliffe and Vogus, 2003)

It is the flexibility and capacity across the organization to handle adversity that give it, and its members, resilience. Others suggest that the problems in defining what is actually meant by resilience, combined with the difficulties in researching it, make for a complex but nonetheless potentially useful concept (Luthar *et al*, 2000).

Leadership challenge

How resilient do you consider yourself to be? Reflect on an experience of adversity. What do you think you have learned through it? How do you think it has strengthened you to face challenges in the future? What steps can you take to develop resilience across your organization?

More help

Key reference

Reivich, K and Shatte, A (2002) *The Resilience Factor*, Broadway Books, New York

Other references

Clough, P, Earle, K and Strycharczyk, D (2008) Developing resilience through coaching, in *Psychometrics in Coaching*, ed J Passmore, Kogan Page, London

Garmezy, N (1973) Competence and adaptation in adult schizophrenic patients and children at risk, in *Schizophrenia: The First Ten Dean Award Lectures*, ed S R Dean, pp 163–204, MSS Information Corporation, New York

Lewis, S (2011) *Positive Psychology at Work*, 1st edn, Wiley-Blackwell, Oxford

Luthar, S S, Cicchetti, D and Becker, B (2000) The construct of resilience: a critical evaluation and guidelines for future work, *Child Development*, **71** (3), pp 543–62

Margolis, J D and Stoltz, P G (2010) How to bounce back from adversity, *Harvard Business Review*, **88** (1–2), pp 86–92

Sutcliffe, K and Vogus, T (2003) Organizing for resilience, in *Positive Organizational Scholarship: Foundations of a New Discipline*, ed K S Cameron, J E Dutton and R E Quinn, pp 94–110, Berrett-Koehler, San Francisco

Tugade, M M and Fredrickson, B L (2004) Resilient individuals use positive emotions to bounce back from negative emotional experiences, *Journal of Personality and Social Psychology*, **86** (2), pp 320–33

Werner, E E and Smith, R S (1982) *Vulnerable but Invincible: A longitudinal study of resilient children and youth*, McGraw-Hill, New York

PART TWO
Team effort

What helps people pull together?

Team working is now so commonplace that leaders can perhaps be for-given for thinking that staff know what's expected of them. They also tend to assume that they will get better results and greater commitment as people work together towards achieving business goals. This second part of the book unpacks some of the assumptions leaders have about the dynamics of people working together.

Motivating teams

The theories we have picked suggest that in groups or teams people's moti-vations change. As people observe and relate to others, something happens about the way they see themselves and their managers. Understanding these shifts in attitude is a key to helping people work well together. Things are seldom as simple as they seem and the psychological dynamics that develop within groups and between groups can appear baffling. We've selected models and ideas that we think help bring clarity and practical help when handling complex human relationships.

Roles

Research indicates that people enjoy taking on particular roles when they join a group. But how can the right people with the right skills be matched with the most-needed roles? It's this type of leadership dilemma that is the focus of one of the models. Another offers ideas about how to make your recruitment processes more reliable so that you end up recruiting the most suitable people to join a team.

Relationships

Making decisions, negotiating the best outcomes and ensuring that everyone is pulling their weight are all important aspects of team life. Every team is different but all face the challenge of getting these things right. With strong positive relationships and supportive management processes, every team stands a good chance of success. This part of the book looks at some of the theories that give practical help in understanding the human aspects of team development and how to handle them.

Your leadership

It's more than likely that you will be leading a team and be a member of several others. Fulfilling your roles and responsibilities brings with it both challenges and the potential to make a major impact on business outcomes. Your own understanding of teams and how they impact on your perform-ance as a leader, we think is critical. Leading people, in our eyes, is not just about performance, but also about helping you make a positive difference to the human experience of team life for everyone.

Do people work harder if you give them more attention?

23

The Hawthorne effect

The big idea

The term 'Hawthorne effect' was coined by psychologist Henry Landsberger (Landsberger, 1958) in the 1950s to summarize what he saw as a key finding of research undertaken at the Hawthorne works of the Western Electric Company near Chicago, Illinois (1924–36). One of the conclusions of the Hawthorne team, led by Harvard social scientist Elton Mayo, was that workers improve their performance when they are being studied, regardless of any type of experimental protocol. In other words, the more attention given to people the more productive they will be. This is the proposition that has become known as the Hawthorne effect. Subsequently, this effect has been assumed to be universally applicable and management training frequently uses the idea to promote the belief that performance will improve in any work context if staff are given sufficent attention. The research was originally published in *Management and the Worker* and contained a number of significant insights which were considered to be, for the 1930s, a radical departure from the then accepted belief that if you get the physical environment right the workforce will inevitably be productive (Roethlisberger and Dickson, 1939).

The Hawthorne experiments initially focused on testing the impact of altering lighting levels on worker output and then moved on to assessing the impact of flexing monetary incentives. These became known as the Relay Test Room studies. The Mica Splitting Test Room studies looked at the effect of altering working conditions, except for pay incentives, on worker performance, and the Bank Wiring Observation Room study looked at the behaviour of people. A major interview programme of 21,000 staff at the plant completed the Hawthorne studies.

Some of the key findings of the studies included the complex nature of the social structure of work groups and the range of impacts this will have on work. Researchers also noted the different attitudes and behaviours of individuals and how they became part of fluid informal groups that were neither designed nor controlled by managers. These groups could exert pressure and encourage people to work at the pace of the group rather than according to individual aptitude. The researchers concluded that there was a social structure in the organization alongside the formal managerial structure. To a 21st-century reader these insights sound basic but at the time they were a paradigm shift in people's understanding of the nature of work, motivation and organizations.

So what?

Aside from the Hawthorne effect, the studies created a major new school of thought about work and workers that became known as the human relations movement. The focus of organizational theorists and psychologists interested in the productivity of people shifted towards exploring how people felt about work and the people they worked with. More interest began to be expressed in how to understand individual personalities and the types of interpersonal skill that supervisors needed to get the best out of people. It became accepted that you could train people to relate better and so create a more conducive and productive workplace. There was also a recognition that economic inducements were not the only means of motivating people. One commentator remarked in the 1980s that the human relations approach 'underlies current attempts by American industry to motivate workers and increase productivity by redesigning job conditions' (Rice, 1982). The growth of interest more recently in emotional intelligence and executive coaching can also ultimately be traced back to the work of Mayo and his team at the Hawthorne works.

What else?

The actual existence of the Hawthorne effect has been seriously questioned by researchers for many years. The loudest voices have been those that have argued that the entire Hawthorne project was deeply flawed. The reasons they give for this are that the researchers:

- did not collect the right sort of data to validate their claims, nor did they use satisfactory analytical methods on the data they did collect;

- focused heavily on group decision-making processes, often ignoring the role of the individual;
- viewed conflict as always destructive and sometimes labelled those who exhibited resistance to them or to work supervisors as unbalanced individuals;
- came with a clear agenda and philosophy that they strongly advocated regardless of any evidence to the contrary.

(Furnham, 2005)

Much criticism has been targeted at the Hawthorne effect itself, with some describing it, and the studies, as a fable (Gale, 2004), as a myth (Rice, 1982), a result of capitalist bias among modern psychologists (Bramel and Friend, 1981) and an urban legend (Kompier, 2006). Among academics there is little support for the reality of the Hawthorne effect but there is recognition that, as an idea, it does have an attraction that keeps it in the mind of managers. Kompier suggests that this is because it's part of a very intriguing set of myths and stories surrounding the Hawthorne project, that it connects powerfully with the beliefs that social relationships really do matter and that human beings are important and worth paying attention to as individuals (Kompier, 2006).

Before we write off the Hawthorne effect completely, a recently published research paper claims to have rediscovered 'lost' data from the original Relay Test Room experiments and suggests that there is now 'weak evidence consistent with more subtle manifestations of Hawthorne effects in the data' (Levitt and List, 2009).

Leadership challenge

Think about what assumptions you have about how people become more productive. Think also about what helps motivate you. How do your assumptions and experiences influence how you develop the people in your team?

More help

Key references

Roethlisberger, F J and Dickson, W J (1939) *Management and the Worker*, Harvard University Press, Boston

Levitt, S D and List, J (2009) *Was There Really a Hawthorne Effect at the Hawthorne Plant? An Analysis of the Original Illumination Experiments*, National Bureau of Economic Research, Cambridge, MA

Rice, B (1982) The Hawthorne defect: persistence of a flawed theory, *Psychology Today*, **16** (2), pp 70–4

Other references

Bramel, D and Friend, R (1981) Hawthorne, the myth of the docile worker, and class bias in psychology, *American Psychologist*, **36** (8), pp 867–78

Furnham, A (2005) *The Psychology of Behaviour at Work: The individual in the organization*, Psychology Press, Hove, Sussex

Gale, E (2004) The Hawthorne studies – a fable for our times? *QJMed*, **97** (7), pp 439–49

Kompier, M A J (2006) The 'Hawthorne effect' is a myth, but what keeps the story going? *Scandinavian Journal of Work Environment and Health*, **32** (5), pp 402–12

Landsberger, H A (1958) *Hawthorne Revisited: Management and the worker, its critics, and developments in human relations in industry*, Cornell University Press, New York

24

Do the assumptions that managers have about people affect how they do their work?

Theory X and Theory Y

The big idea

At the heart of Theory X and Theory Y is the proposition that the assumptions managers have about how other people think and behave at work will directly impact on their management style. Douglas McGregor, an American psychologist, theorized that managers with a Theory X orientation will assume that the average member of staff will dislike work and therefore need to be threatened with punishment and cajoled into working towards achieving organizational objectives. This mindset is likely to give rise to an authoritarian and controlling set of behaviours. On the other hand, a manager with a Theory Y orientation assumes that people naturally want to do a good job, are keen to take responsibility for what they do and see work as leading to self-fulfilment. The type of managerial behaviour that naturally follows is trusting, openly communicative, supportive and collaborative in style. McGregor's argument is that behaviour derives from these assumptions and that they tend to be self-fulfilling both in the way a manager behaves and the response of the employees to that behaviour.

McGregor set out his thesis in a seminal work, *The Human Side of Enterprise* (McGregor, 1960). The model is well known and has been cited as one of the principal foundations of modern organizational development (Sorensen and Minahan, 2011). Although the theory is often presented as two entirely separate concepts, X and Y, McGregor never intended them to be viewed as such. They are not two ends of one spectrum, since it is possible for a manager to hold both sets of assumptions and apply them towards different individuals or in different situations in one way or another according to their interpretation of the situation (Warner Burke, 2011).

McGregor used his theory to challenge managers to reflect on their assumptions and then behave in ways that encouraged the full utilization of the human potential within the organization. He believed that this would only be possible through a Theory Y set of behaviours. To underline this, he used 'hard' words like 'self-centred', 'indolent', 'gullible' to describe people in Theory X while in Theory Y he talked of people having a range of needs, which reflects the admiration he had for the work of Abraham Maslow. People, he believed, hoped to satisfy the need for self-fullfilment through their participation in the work of a supportive organization (McGregor, 1960).

So what?

McGregor's thesis has been credited with spawning a whole set of ideas and organizational practices that have become so common that most people now take them for granted. Here are some of them:

- Leadership and managerial behaviours can be categorized and used as the basis for developing management skills (previously the dominant assumption was that managers were 'born and not made').
- Managers should put in time and effort to create a supportive environment in which the skills and commitment of employees can be 'drawn out'. This can be achieved, for example, through job-enrichment strategies and enabling a high degree of employee autonomy.
- Emphasizing the criticality of excellent team working in the achievement of organizational goals. For McGregor this meant frequent discussions about goals, everyone knowing what their team objectives were, and consensus decision making (McGregor, 1960).
- Employee diversity should be seen as a major advantage for an organization.
- The widespread adoption of 'management by objectives' which he championed alongside Peter Drucker.
- Decentralization as the organizational form that best supports employee involvement.

Of particular significance is the notion of participative management, which has become an all-pervasive, globally accepted style of engaging employees in their work and the future of their company (Sorensen and Minahan, 2011).

What else?

Few people talk explicitly about Theory X and Theory Y in management conversations today. However, the influence of McGregor in understanding motivation, behaviour and the way organizations can be managed should not be underestimated. There has been empirical research undertaken on many of aspects of Theory Y in particular (for example, Harung and Travis, 2011; Kopelman, Prottas and Falk, 2010; and Sager, 2008). They all confirm the validity of McGregor's initial theoretical constructs. Recently, scholars (Sorensen and Minahan, 2011) have linked McGregor's ideas with the emergence of appreciative inquiry (AI), a significant organizational development process, whose positive approach to the future and underpinning belief in self-fulfilling prophecies echo those of McGregor.

Leadership challenge

What assumptions do you make about how others are thinking and working in your team? What impact does this have on your own leadership behaviour?

More help

Key references

Carson, C M (2005) A historical view of Douglas McGregor's Theory Y, *Management Decision*, **43** (3), pp 450–60

McGregor, D (1960) *The Human Side of Enterprise*, McGraw-Hill, New York

Sorensen, P F and Minahan, M (2011) McGregor's legacy: the evolution and current application of Theory Y management, *Journal of Management History*, **17** (2), pp 178–92

Other references

Harung, H S and Travis, F (2011) Higher mind–brain development in successful leaders: testing a unified theory of performance, *Cognitive Processing*, **12**, pp 1–11

Head, T C (2011) Douglas McGregor's legacy: lessons learned, lessons lost, *Journal of Management History*, **17** (2), pp 202–16

Kopelman, R E, Prottas, D J and Falk, D W (2010) Construct validation of a theory X/Y behavior scale, *Leadership and Organization Development Journal*, **31** (2), pp 120–35

Russ, T L (2011) Theory X/Y assumptions as predictors of managers' propensity for participative decision making, *Management Decision*, **49** (5), pp 823–36

Sager, K L (2008) An exploratory study of the relationships between theory X/Y assumptions and superior communicator style, *Management Communication Quarterly*, **22** (2), pp 288–312

Schein, E (2011) Douglas McGregor: theoretician, moral philosopher or behaviorist? An analysis of the interconnections between assumptions, values and behavior, *Journal of Management History*, **17** (2), pp 156–64

Warner Burke, W (2011) On the legacy of Theory Y, *Journal of Management History*, **17** (2), pp 193–201

25

Do groups always make the best decisions?

Groupthink

The big idea

Groupthink is thought to have been first coined by social psychologist Irving Janis in 1971 (Janis, 1971). It has since entered the popular vocabulary and is often used as a shorthand explanation of why a particular group made a poor decision. In his original article Janis views the term as:

> a quick and easy way to refer to the mode of thinking that persons engage in when concurrence-seeking becomes so dominant in a cohesive ingroup that it tends to override realistic appraisal of alternative courses of action.
>
> (Janis, 1971: 443)

He came to the conclusion that groupthink existed through researching mainly historical records of political and military events specifically looking for evidence of how group dynamics appeared to impact on the final decision. Notable studies included the Bay of Pigs, the lack of preparedness by the United States for the Pearl Harbour attacks and the escalation of the Vietnam war.

Janis describes the characteristics of groupthink in a group as:

- *An illusion of invulnerability*. People become over-optimistic about the situation they are confronted with and are happy to take unjustifiable risks.
- *Belief in the rectitude of the group*. Members of the group think that they are morally correct in their views.
- *Negative views of competitors*. A tendency to be disparaging about the leaders of the opposing side.
- *Sanctity of group consensus*. People become very hesitant about voicing their own opinion when it contradicts what they perceive to be the view of the group.

- *Illusion of unanimity*. The group presents to outsiders the perception that everyone was in agreement with the decision when, in reality, they may not be.
- *Erecting a protective shield*. The group defends itself against alternative perspectives presented by outsiders.

He also suggested that there are a number of antecedents that may predispose a group to groupthink. These include close relationships between group members, a powerful leader who takes sides, members lacking confidence and a significant external threat to the group and/or those it represents.

Some of the problems resulting from groupthink that Janis identified include the failure to consider a full range of options, not enough questioning of proposed solutions, unwillingness to evaluate information impartially and little or no planning for predictable setbacks.

So what?

In a later book Janis suggested that there are a number of ways groups can avoid the pitfalls of groupthink. These include:

- encouraging evaluation of what is being proposed by group members and the leader being willing to accept criticism;
- the leader holding back from expressing their preference until the end of the debate;
- identifying one member of the group to be a 'devil's advocate' and deliberately challenge conclusions;
- exposing potential solutions to outsiders for them to critique;
- breaking meetings into subgroups to consider different aspects of proposals.

(Janis, 1982)

While all these seem eminently sensible, a truism about groupthink appears to be that groups are not aware of it happening until they look back in retrospect and then conclude that it was groupthink that made them act that way! On the other hand, if a group succeeds in a task they are likely to ascribe this not to groupthink but rather to synergy or excellent teamwork and leadership. It could be argued, therefore, that groupthink is a way of labelling poor group decisions.

What else?

There are, perhaps unsurprisingly, plenty of criticisms of Janis's concept. Baron, for example, highlights the absence of sufficient empirical studies that test out the key linkages between group relations and the quality of decision making

(Baron, 2005). Baron goes on to argue that in more mundane, everyday decision-making contexts than, say, going to war, the antecedent conditions for groupthink may be triggers other than those considered by Janis. This view strengthens the case for presenting a revised model of groupthink. Other theorists similarly present their own revision of the model. Aldag and Fuller comment that:

> evaluation indicates that research does not provide convincing support for the validity of the groupthink phenomenon or for the suggestion that groupthink characteristics lead to negative outcomes.

(1993: 533)

Their alternative model focuses on group decision-making processes.

Neck and Manz (1994) see that self-managing teams might be vulnerable to groupthink and propose what they view as a more positive synergistic process called 'teamthink'.

Among researchers there is very little consensus about the validity of Janis's model of groupthink. However, it and other derivative models continue to be popular among management theorists and managers who have a practical interest in how to improve the quality of decision making in the boardroom.

Leadership challenge

Given the ideas of Janis, how do you encourage challenging voices in your own team?

More help

Key references

Janis, I L (1971) Groupthink, *Psychology Today*, November, pp 443–7, American Psychological Association
Janis, I L (1982) *Groupthink: Psychological studies of policy decisions and fiascoes*, Houghton Mifflin, Boston

Other references

Aldag, R J and Fuller, S R (1993) Beyond fiasco: a reappraisal of the groupthink phenomenon and a new model of group decision processes, *Psychological Bulletin*, **113** (3), pp 533–52
Baron, R S (2005) So right it's wrong: groupthink and the ubiquitous nature of polarized group decision making, *Advances in Experimental Social Psychology*, **37**, pp 219–53
Neck, C P and Manz, C C (1994) From groupthink to teamthink: toward the creation of constructive thought patterns in self-managing work teams, *Human Relations*, **47** (8), pp 929–52

26

What behaviours improve team performance?

Belbin team roles

The big idea

In the 1970s Dr Meredith Belbin did research to identify the factors that influence team performance. At the outset his assumption was that teams with higher intelligence scores would outperform the less intelligent. This proved to be wrong. Using observational techniques on MBA students at Henley Management College (UK) over a seven-year period, he found instead that a range of other criteria had a greater bearing on team success. He discovered that determinants of high performance include the need for team members to perform a technical role as well as support the wider work of the team. It is also helpful if there is an optimal balance between the relative strengths of team members and the nature of the tasks they need to accomplish.

Belbin, however, became most well known for his observations that successful teams need people to play specific roles and that personality, behavioural preferences and mental abilities lead some people to prefer to play particular roles in a team and not others. The implication is that some teams can be unbalanced, with critical roles unfilled, while others achieve success because all team roles are occupied by people skilled in performing them (Belbin, 1981).

Building on his observations, Belbin created a typology of roles that need to be fulfilled in a high-performing team. While some of the role names have changed over the years, and one additional role (Specialist) added to the original eight, the descriptors have remained broadly the same (Table 26.1). These descriptors are short summaries to give a flavour of each role. More information is available on the Belbin Associates website: **http://www.belbin.com**.

TABLE 26.1   Belbin team roles

Role	Descriptor
Shaper	Dynamic individuals who are focused on the task and will encourage others to do the same. They can be argumentative.
Implementer	People who turn ideas into action using an organized and systematic approach. Sometimes resistant to change and inflexible.
Completer/Finisher	Focused on achieving the end result, these people helpfully pay much attention to detail. They can be prone to anxiety and find delegation difficult.
Coordinator	Often identified as the natural leader, they are calm and supportive of others. Sometimes they can be prone to over-delegate and may be considered manipulative by others.
Team worker	Natural negotiators who help the team work together. They are flexible in their approach to work but can be indecisive.
Resource investigator	People who are innovative and curious. Using their networks and contacts, they will try to access resources to help the team. They can be seen as over-optimistic at times.
Plant	Very creative, always keen to explore new ideas. They can be poor at communicating with team members.
Monitor–evaluator	Good at assessing other people's ideas and identifying the best way to do things. Can appear detached and reactive rather than taking the initiative.
Specialist	Focuses on their technical contribution to achieving the task but may tend not to see the bigger picture.

It is worth noting that each role has associated with it potential weaknesses as well as behavioural and attitudinal strengths. These weaknesses are considered allowable since they also bring with them much-needed positive strengths. Belbin emphasizes that the roles are not about personality traits but specifically concerned with describing observable behaviours.

The consequence is that one person may perfectly feasibly demonstrate the behaviours associated with several roles within a team. It also means that people are able to adapt their behaviours to meet the requirements of the tasks facing a team rather than being locked into a relatively fixed pattern of relating and performing. This perspective is reflected in the definition of team role: 'a pattern of behaviour characteristic of the way in which one team member interacts with another where his performance serves to facilitate the progress of the team as a whole' (Belbin, 1981).

So what?

The most well known practical application of the theory is Belbin's Team Role Self-Perception Inventory (BTRSPI). This copyrighted questionnaire enables team members to identify which set/s of role behaviours they believe they exhibit. It is available for individuals and teams via the Belbin Associates website. Included in the package is the option of asking up to six colleagues for their observations of team behaviour. This provides a 360° feedback report alongside the self-report. Other materials to support team development, such as books, videos and games, are also available.

The BTRSPI is used by organizations for a wide range of purposes. Team formation and development are the obvious one, but there are many examples of it being used in job selection processes and promotion assessment centres. Where it is used developmentally, experience suggests that it opens up helpful conversations about how a team functions and how, through appropriate role behaviours, it can achieve more.

What else?

The validity and reliability of the BTRSPI as a psychological test have been the subject of considerable debate. Research published in 1993 suggested that the types of question used in the test and the lack of a verifiable psychological theory mean that the inventory does not statistically measure what it claims (Furnham *et al*, 1993). Belbin responded by arguing that the inventory is a tool for teams and management consultants and was never intended to be a conventional psychometric test. Following some minor redesign of the inventory, relatively recent research indicates that the BTRSPI is a much more reliable psychological instrument than was originally thought (Swailes and McIntyre-Bhatty, 2002). Some psychologists remain perplexed at the continuing popularity of the BTRSPI when they believe its underpinning assumptions are false (Furnham, 2005).

Leadership challenge

What Belbin role do you most frequently adopt? Why not try something different at your next team meeting? What roles are missing from your team? How might you change that?

More help

http://www.belbin.com/

Key reference

Belbin, R (1981) *Management Teams: Why they succeed or fail*, Elsevier, London

Other references

Furnham, A (2005) *The Psychology of Behaviour at Work: The individual in the organization*, Psychology Press, Hove, Sussex

Furnham, A, Steele, H, Pendleton, D *et al* (1993) A psychometric assessment of the Belbin team-role self-perception inventory. Author's reply. *Journal of Occupational and Organizational Psychology*, **66** (3), pp 245–61

Swailes, S and McIntyre-Bhatty, T (2002) The 'Belbin' team role inventory: reinterpreting reliability estimates, *Journal of Managerial Psychology*, **17** (6), pp 529–36

Does an attractive communicator influence our decision making?

27

Attractiveness theory

The big idea

An understanding of why and how people change their minds has been of considerable interest to psychologists since the 1930s. Understandably, business psychologists have had a strong interest in this, both from the perspective of helping managers and leaders gain insight into how to persuade staff to work smarter and also how to influence consumers more effectively to buy products.

A review of the literature indicates that there is no one 'big idea' but a number offering a variety of insights, some with a research base, others theories waiting to be tested. We will focus here on the idea that the attractiveness of the communicator can change attitudes.

The 1950s saw some influential thinking, with Tannenbaum (1956) claiming that the degree of attitude change is directly related to the degree of perceived attractiveness of the individual (change agent). There is also a suggestion that the extent of the power of the attractiveness was correlated with the desire of the receiver of the message to be like the person communicating with them. We only have to look at media adverts to see how this notion has become the tool of choice of advertisers as they seek to tap into the aspirations of consumers. Some research by Mills and Aronson (1965) found that while attractiveness is useful when the message is unpopular, its power can be undone if the messenger is perceived to be covertly exploiting their attractiveness.

In the early 1970s Dion and others undertook a piece of research which concluded that a physical attractiveness stereotype does exist and that those who are perceived to be more physically attractive are also perceived to possess more socially desirable personalities than others (Dion, Berscheid and Walster, 1972). Shelly Chaiken published the results of research which found that one group of participants used high levels of cognitive effort to draw a conclusion about an argument while the second group tended to be more persuaded by other factors such as the identity (and by implication the attractiveness) of the message giver rather than the substance of the argument (Chaiken, 1980).

Earlier work by Chaiken found that a communicator deemed attractive stood more chance of persuading people of the value of an undesirable message than an unattractive communicator. She also demonstrated that people persuaded cognitively by strong arguments are more likely to hold their new views for a longer time than those primarily influenced by the attractiveness or otherwise of the messenger (Chaiken, 1979).

In the early 1980s Petty, Cacioppo and Goldman (1981) proposed the Elaboration Likelihood Model, which holds that there are two routes through which people are persuaded. The first is the 'central route', where arguments are presented to the receiver who scrutinizes the information carefully. It is assumed that the receiver is able to analyse information and is personally interested in the topic. The second route is the 'peripheral route', which focuses the receiver on anything but the core message. Celebrity endorsements, attractive images and music play a major role in persuading people to be interested in the topic. The assumption is that people are less interested in and concerned about the issue than those who are participating in the central route. It is therefore important for the messengers to understand what tools they need to use to get to people through either or both routes. The model also indicates that those persuaded through the 'peripheral route' are likely to hold to their views for a shorter period of time than those persuaded through the 'central route'. Subsequent research by Kahle and Homer (1985) suggested that physical attractiveness is communicated more speedily than other types of information and is treated as information that supports social adaptation (people's ability to adjust to living within socially accepted norms).

So what?

A review by Benoy of the research in this area concluded that evidence supports the idea that physically attractive communicators are more generally liked (Benoy, 1982). While they may also have an impact on attitude change, it will probably be by supporting, for example, better recognition of an advertisement. Interestingly, the studies show consistently that attractiveness in itself does not assure any audience that the communicator is expert on the topic they are speaking about. However, research in this area is not definitive in its findings, especially when it comes to confirming the connection between attractiveness and persuasion. There are many other factors which are likely to impact on how attitudes change, which may have more to do with social norms, gender differences, economic pressures and even racial stereotyping. Much of the research work has concentrated on building a body of knowledge about marketing and advertising psychology. As yet, no research appears to have focused specifically on the perceived attractiveness, or otherwise, of managers, and their effectiveness in influencing staff, although there is research on the impact of height (for men) on salary levels (taller men get paid more) (Judge and Cable, 2004) and also on wearing glasses (men with glasses are considered smarter and harder working) (Harris, Harris and Bochner, 1982).

What else?

There are plenty of criticisms of the research, ranging from the lack of clear definitions of 'physical attractiveness' to the use of the unspecific concept of 'likeability' by some researchers. Much of the research appears to have used quite socially narrow groups, for example young students studying marketing, and this probably means that results are not representative of a much more diverse general population. Aspects of the notion of attractiveness are quite controversial as public statements, as was demonstrated in 2011 by Dr Satoshi Kanazawa of the London School of Economics (**http://www.bbc.co.uk/news/uk-13452699**) about the relative attractiveness of one racial group compared to another. Tread with care is the message!

The answer to the question of what influences our attitudes goes way beyond the potential impact of attractiveness on us as individuals. Losada and Heaphy (2004) support the positive psychology perspective that the degree of connectivity between individuals in a work team, combined with positive, affirming talk, will have a direct impact on measurable performance. Other recent schools of thought (Gergen, 2001) argue that our experiences and attitudes are socially constructed among us rather than just the result of individuals being persuaded of a point of view.

Leadership challenge

Get some feedback on your style of communication. How can you enhance the impact of your communication through thinking about the non-verbal messages you give?

More help

Key references

Etcoff, N (1999) *Survival of the Prettiest*, Random House, New York

Chaiken, S (1979) Communicator physical attractiveness and persuasion, *Journal of Personality and Social Psychology*, **37** (8), pp 1387–97

Gergen, K J (2001) Psychological science in a postmodern context, *American Psychologist*, **56** (10), pp 803–13

Losada, M and Heaphy, E (2004) The role of positivity and connectivity in the performance of business teams: a nonlinear dynamics model, *American Behavioral Scientist*, **47** (6), pp 740–65

Mills, J and Aronson, E (1965) Opinion change as a function of the communicator's attractiveness and desire to influence, *Journal of Personality and Social Psychology*, **1** (2), pp 173–7

Tannenbaum, P (1956) Initial attitude toward source and concept as factors in attitude change through communication, *Public Opinion Quarterly*, **20**, pp 413–26

Other references

Benoy, J W (1982) The credibility of physically attractive communicators: a review, *Journal of Advertising*, **11** (3), pp 15–24

Chaiken, S (1980) Heuristic versus systematic information processing and the use of source versus message cues in persuasion, *Journal of Personality and Social Psychology*, **39** (5), pp 752–66

Dion, K, Berscheid, E and Walster, E (1972) What is beautiful is good, *Journal of Personality and Social Psychology*, **24** (3), pp 285–90

Harris, M B, Harris, R J and Bochner, S (1982) Fat, four-eyed, and female: stereotypes of obesity, glasses and gender, *Journal of Applied Social Psychology*, **12**, pp 503–16

Kahle, L R and Homer, P M (1985) Physical attractiveness of the celebrity endorser: a social adaptation perspective, *Journal of Consumer Research*, **11** (4), pp 954–61

Losada, M and Heaphy, E (2004) The role of positivity and connectivity in the performance of business teams, *American Behavioral Scientist*, **47** (6), pp 740–65

Petty, R E, Cacioppo, J T and Goldman, R (1981) Personal involvement as a determinant of argument-based persuasion, *Journal of Personality and Social Psychology*, **41** (5), pp 847–55

Judge, T A and Cable, D A (2004) The effect of physical height on workplace success and income: preliminary test of a theoretical model, *Journal of Applied Psychology*, **89** (3), pp 428–41

How to use goal setting to enhance performance

28

Goal-setting theory

The big idea

Goal setting is a simple process and many of us do it much of the time. It involves establishing a clear outcome at the start of any task that defines what will be achieved at the end point of the task. This outcome may be defined as a SMART goal – SMART stands for specific, measurable, achievable, realistic and time-targeted.

While this appears to be a simple process, there is a significant amount of research which tells us both that goal setting is good for us and how to set goals that work.

The goal-setting theory was developed by Locke from a series of studies undertaken during the mid-1960s (Locke and Bryan, 1966). Locke's work was seeking to explain human actions in specific work situations. The original model consisted of five steps: step 1: environmental stimuli; step 2: cognition; step 3: evaluation; step 4: intentions/goal setting; step 5: performance. The theory argues that goals and intentions are cognitive and wilful and that they serve as mediators of human actions. Further, our needs and our goals are mediated by our values and beliefs.

Subsequent research in this field has been led by Edwin Locke and Gary Latham, with scores of publications exploring the application of the theory (see, for example, Latham and Locke, 2002). In one example Locke and colleagues examined the behavioural effects of goal setting and concluded that 90 per cent of laboratory and field studies involving specific and challenging goals resulted in higher levels of performance than if no goals had been set (Locke *et al*, 1981).

The two most important findings of the theory are, first, that setting specific (SMART) goals generates higher levels of performance than setting vaguely defined goals, and second, the more challenging the goal the harder the person will work. However, such potential influences on performance are affected by two issues. First, individuals aspiring towards a goal need regular and detailed feedback. Second, the person working towards the goal must be committed to achieving the specific goal.

Of all the models in this book, goal-setting theory may be the most important and most practical. At least, this was the view of the Academy of Management, which in a review of psychology models ranked goal-setting theory as number 1 in importance out of 73 management theories (Miner, 2003). Others have ranked it number 1 in practical utility compared with hundreds of management theories (Lee and Earley, 1992).

So what?

If the aim of the manager is both to develop the individual and to assist them in enhancing their work performance, what types of goals are most effective for realizing these aims? The research evidence from a wide range of workplace studies gives us clear guidance in this area (see Passmore, 2003).

First, the goals should be as challenging as possible, while remaining achievable (Locke and Latham, 1990). In practical terms, goals can be made highly challenging as long as the individual is committed to achieving them and they have the ability to do so. The latter point is the more difficult to assess. It is affected not only by the individual's past performance and awareness of their own ability but also by the manager's understanding of the skills required for the successful completion of the task, the time taken to develop these and the demands of the business environment.

Second, the goal set should be highly specific (Locke and Latham, 1990). The more precisely the goal is defined the clearer the shared understanding between manager and individual about what needs to be achieved. This is likely to mean a quantifiable measure of performance for a specific task, by a due date; to sell, for example, 50 mobile phones during the third quarter, as measured by the sales ledger on 31 December.

Third, goal commitment is a critical element of goal realization. Goals ideally should have a personal meaning for the individual. If the manager discusses a goal in detail with an employee, more intensive cognitive processing is likely to occur, resulting in a higher likelihood of the goal being realized (Gollwitzer, Heckhausen and Ratajczak, 1990). The individual also needs to believe in their own ability to achieve the goal. This can be done by the manager supporting them to develop new behaviours, task strategies, skills training or by the manager expressing expectations of their ability to perform at this new level. For the goal to be realizable, the individual must both understand why the goal is of value and believe that they can achieve it.

Fourth, long-range goals impact on the degree of commitment over time (Lerner and Locke, 1995). By establishing goals with milestones at medium-term intervals, progress can be tracked. Long-term goals can allow a number of medium-term goals to be woven together to create a longer-term vision and assist in maintaining persistence of action over time.

What else?

Like all approaches, goal-setting theory has its limitations. In a business, the goals identified by an individual manager may not strictly align with the goals of the organization. As a result, the goals of the manager may come into direct conflict with the organization. This requires effective goal setting to be a negotiated process between the individual and their senior manager, thus ensuring both personal commitment to the goals and alignment with wider organizational priorities.

A second issue is that in complex environments, most frequently found in government, goal setting may actually impair perceived performance. In these situations, an individual may become solely preoccupied with meeting goals, rather than maintaining vital relationships and performing the necessarily diverse range of allied tasks. In a complex organizational context, *how* a goal is met can be almost as important as achieving it. Finally, an over-emphasis on specific goals can narrow down learning opportunities and the potential for wider exploration of an issue.

Leadership challenge

Write yourself a one-page life plan for the coming 12 months. What would you like to achieve by the end of the next 365 days at work, in your family relationships, in sport, travel and hobbies? Produce a mind map of your goals and stick it inside your wardrobe.

More help

Key references

Latham, G and Locke, E (2002) Building a practically useful theory of goal setting and task motivation, *The American Psychologist*, 57 (9), pp 705–17

Locke, E, Shaw, K, Saari, L *et al* (1981) Goal setting and task performance: 1969–1980, *Psychological Bulletin*, **90** (1), pp 125–52

Locke, E A and Latham, G P (1990) *A Theory of Goal Setting and Task Performance*, Prentice-Hall, New York

Other references

Gollwitzer, P, Heckhausen, H and Ratajczak, K (1990) From weighing to willing: approaching a change decision through pre or post decisional mentation, *Organizational Behaviour and Human Decision Processes*, **45** (1), pp 41–65

Latham, G and Locke, E (1991) Self regulating through goal setting, *Organizational Behaviour and Human Decision Processes*, **50** (2), pp 212–47

Locke, E A and Bryan, J F (1966) The effects of goal-setting, rule-learning, and knowledge of score on performance, *American Journal of Psychology*, **79**, pp 451–7

Lee, C and Earley, P (1992) Comparative peer evaluations of organizational behavior theories, *Organizational Development Journal*, **10**, pp 37–42

Lerner, B S and Locke, E A (1995) The effect of goal setting, self-efficacy, competition, and personal trials on the performance of an endurance task, *Journal of Sport and Exercise Psychology*, **17** (2) pp 138–52

Miner, J B (2003) The rated importance, scientific validity, and practical usefulness of organizational behavior theories: a quantitative review, *Academy of Management Learning and Education*, **2**, pp 250–68

Passmore, J (2003) Goal-focused coaching, *The Occupational Psychologist – Special Issue: Coaching Psychology*, **49**, 30–3

Why do people obey authority figures even when they are being asked to do something they know is wrong?

29

Obedience to authority theory

The big idea

Between 1961 and 1962 social psychologist Stanley Milgram conducted a series of famous, or infamous, experiments at Yale University. He wanted to find out how far a human being will go in hurting another human being when instructed to do so by an authority figure. Subsequently, writers have suggested that his main concern was to understand the nature of obedience to authority. While this is true, Milgram himself was intrigued by the Nazis and the way they were able to command apparently ordinary moral people to commit the Holocaust.

His experiments involved recruiting 40 local males to attend a purpose-built laboratory. They were told that little was known about the effect of punishment on learning and that the experiment was about how to improve education. One of the two participants present at each experiment would take the role of teacher and the other the learner. It was always fixed that the recruit would take on the role of teacher while an actor would be the learner. A supervisor would tell the 'teacher' what to do. The instruction to the 'teacher' was that if a wrong answer was given to a memory test question, a shock of 15 volts had to be administered using the panel of switches in front of them. The next time a wrong answer was given a shock of 30 v was required, up to a maximum 450 v. To make the 'teacher' believe that they were using real electricity, a test shock of 45 v was administered to them.

The 'teacher' could hear the impact on the 'learner' of the shocks they administered, while the experiment supervisor stood by them to instruct them to proceed to the end of the process in spite of any cries of pain and requests by the learner to stop.

A startling finding was that 26 out of the 40 participants were prepared to 'shock' the learner at the maximum 450 v level – which, if really applied, would most likely have resulted in the death of the 'learner'. These results appear to be sustained across group member differences such as education and values. The second major finding was the degree of stress and tension experienced by the 'teacher' participants. This manifested itself in physical shaking and loud emotional cries to stop. Milgram commented that 'Any understanding of the phenomenon of obedience must rest on an analysis of the particular conditions in which it occurs' (Milgram, 1965: 370).

In his book on the experiments he concluded:

Ordinary people, simply doing their jobs, and without any particular hostility on their part, can become agents in a terrible destructive process. Moreover, even when the destructive effects of their work become patently clear, and they are asked to carry out actions incompatible with fundamental standards of morality, relatively few people have the resources needed to resist authority.

(Milgram, 1974)

So what?

Milgram reflected on the experiments and suggested a number of contextual features that may go some way to explaining why people were apparently so willing to override their values and maintain obedience to authority. These features include:

- The apparent respectability of the experiment organizers and their location on a university campus.

- The worthy stated purpose of the experiments to enhance the effectiveness of education.

- The belief that the victim voluntarily submitted to the authority system of the experimenter.

- The obligation that the participant feels towards helping the experimenter complete the process, given that he has also volunteered to take part. There is a contract between them all.

- The lack of time the participant is given to reflect on his actions and the circumstances in which he find himself.

At a more general level, the conflict stems from the opposition of two deeply ingrained behavior dispositions: first, the disposition not to harm other people, and second, the tendency to obey those whom we perceive to be legitimate authorities.

(Milgram, 1965)

While Milgram did not apply these inferences specifically to management in organizations, he did see his work and writings as a means by which the threat from any totalitarian authority system, including managerial ones, could be better understood and countered.

What else?

It is unsurprising that Milgram's experimental protocol has come under serious criticism for both deceiving participants and causing them psychological distress. In today's ethical climate it is very unlikely that he would have received approval to proceed.

One critique of the findings argues that what Milgram observed was not a moral dilemma but rather social awkwardness given the social relationship that had developed between the experimenter and the participant (Sabini and Silver, 1985). It was the participant not knowing how to deal with this awkwardness that led to the apparent obedience Milgram described. The solution, it is suggested, is to train people how to be assertive in the face of authority. Another criticism of the experiments is that Milgram framed obedience as potentially destructive, while others see it as potentially constructively supportive of good social order (Passini and Morselli, 2009).

Since the Milgram experiments, further research on the topic, using more ethical approaches, has been undertaken across cultures and involving women. The conclusion is that obedience rates remain as Milgram observed and that there is no difference in rates between genders (Blass, 1999).

Leadership challenge

How might you strengthen the assertiveness of the people you lead?

More help

Key references

Milgram, S (1965) Some conditions of obedience and disobedience to authority, *Human Relations*, 18, pp 57–76

Milgram, S (1974) *Obedience to Authority*, Harper and Row, New York

Other references

Blass, T (1999) The Milgram paradigm after 35 years: some things we now know about obedience to authority, *Journal of Applied Social Psychology*, **29** (5), pp 55–78

Passini, S and Morselli, D (2009) Authority relationships between obedience and disobedience, *New Ideas in Psychology*, **27** (1), pp 96–106

Sabini, J and Silver, M (1985) Critical thinking and obedience to authority, *National Forum*, **65**, pp 13–17

How can you select the best candidate at an interview?

30

Behavioural interviewing

The big idea

Behavioural interviewing is a technique to improve the reliability of interviews at predicting how well candidates will perform in a job. Historically, job interviews have been seen as notoriously bad at evaluating the suitability of applicants. Given the amount of money and effort at stake if a wrong appointment is made, it's important to get the process right first time.

The basic assumption is that the most accurate prediction of future behaviour is past behaviour in a similar situation. To use behavioural interviewing (sometimes called patterned behaviour description interviewing or PBDI), the interviewer needs to look at the job description in advance and identify the required skills and behaviours associated with the work. This will include, for example, behaviours and traits such as decisiveness, initiative, flexibility, resilience and sensitivity. During the interview the interviewer will then ask the candidate the following questions:

- Describe a situation in which you were under pressure to make a quick decision. What happened and how did you make the decision?
- Give me an example of a time when you used your own initiative to solve a problem.
- Tell me about a time when you handled interpersonal conflict in a team you were leading.

Using a pre-agreed scoring system, the interviewer or panel will rate each candidate's answers according to the extent they have previously demonstrated the required behaviours. This approach gives a degree of objectivity and helps remove personal bias from the process.

Behavioural interviewing forms part of a structured approach to interviewing that has gained popularity over the past three decades. Research by Campion and Barclay confirms that relying less on casual interview conversations and more on well-designed processes and questions enhances reliability and validity of interviews (Campion, Palmer and Campion, 1997; Barclay, 1999). A structured interview may also include situational questions, asking candidates what they might do in certain hypothetical situations, and a formal presentation followed by questions.

So what?

The interviewer

Benefits of using this technique include a degree of flexibility in tailoring questions in response to the candidate's narratives rather than sticking with a set script of questions (Barclay, 2001). It also means that candidates are less able to 'fake it' as they are required to draw upon real experiences rather than hypothetical ones. Because data are recorded, and scores awarded against behaviour descriptions, decisions about a candidate are more likely to be evidence based than otherwise might be the case. This also makes it much easier to give clear and constructive feedback to unsuccessful candidates.

Behavioural interviewing does require a good deal of preparation in attributing behaviours to job descriptions and then formulating good questions. Training is needed to use the technique effectively.

The candidate

If candidates are aware that behavioural interviewing will form part of a recruitment process, and given its popularity it's highly probable, they can prepare in advance. Hints for candidates include:

- reviewing the company website for clues about the type of behaviours they value;
- taking a detailed look at the job description and focusing on behaviours which are mentioned implicitly or explicitly;
- reflecting on past experiences that demonstrate these behaviours;
- using the STAR model to structure behavioural 'stories' in advance of an interview (Table 30.1).
- thinking of stories that start out negatively but end up positively as well as those that are positive all the way through;
- learning to tailor a small number of stories that can be used to evidence a number of behaviours;
- being prepared for the interviewer to probe responses in depth.

TABLE 30.1   The STAR model

Situation	Outline in a couple of sentences the situation/context.
Task	What was the specific task that needed to be accomplished? Avoid generalization and give sufficient detail. It is ok to draw upon tasks from volunteering or at college, providing they are fairly recent and relevant.
Action taken	Be as specific as possible about the behaviours demonstrated while doing the task. Link them back to the behaviour being asked about.
Result	Describe what happened and the outcomes. Add in some numbers, such as additional revenue generated or money saved.

What else?

In recent years there has been a lot of research into the usefulness of interviews. The question is: 'Do interviews help employers select the best person for the job?' The results suggest that they do, but with certain caveats. McDaniel *et al* (1994) found that while unstructured interviews worked, structured interviews, including behavioural and situational interviewing, worked even better. Huffcutt *et al* (2001) found that some behaviours and skills, such as decision making and maintaining good interpersonal relationships, are easier to evaluate in a structured interview than, for example, broad communication skills. Barclay (2001) found that structured interviews were mainly used for management posts and often alongside personality tests. Big corporates particularly liked the approach. Janz, who did the initial development work on patterned behaviour description interviewing, in later research found evidence not only of interviewers' satisfaction with the outcomes, but also higher levels of candidate enjoyment of the interview process when compared with more traditional approaches (Janz, 1982; Janz and Mooney, 1993).

The main limitations of the technique cited by managers are that it is time-consuming to prepare, and requires training and further practice (Barclay, 2001).

Leadership challenge

At the next interviews you chair, design questions which are behaviourally based and then practise using them with candidates. Reflect on how these were useful in the recruitment process.

More help

Key references

Janz, T (1982) Initial comparisons of patterned behavior description interviews versus unstructured interviews, *Journal of Applied Psychology*, **67** (5), pp 577–80

McDaniel, M A, Whetzel, D L, Schmidt, F L *et al* (1994) The validity of employment interviews: a comprehensive review and meta-analysis, *Journal of Applied Psychology*, **79** (4), pp 599–616

Other references

Barclay, J M (1999) Employee selection: a question of structure, *Personnel Review*, **28** (1/2), pp 134–51

Barclay, J M (2001) Improving selection interviews with structure: organizations' use of 'behavioural' interviews, *Personnel Review*, **30** (1), pp 81–101

Campion, M A, Palmer, D K and Campion, J E (1997) A review of structure in the selection interview, *Personnel Psychology*, **50** (3), pp 655–702

Huffcutt, A I, Conway, J M, Roth, P L *et al* (2001) Identification and meta-analytic assessment of psychological constructs measured in employment interviews, *Journal of Applied Psychology*, **86** (5), pp 897–913

Janz, T and Mooney, G (1993) Interviewer and candidate reactions to patterned behaviour description interviews, *International Journal of Selection and Assessment*, **1** (3), pp 165–9

Majority and minority influence

The big idea

Majority and minority influence theories are two related ideas about how people in a social context can be persuaded to change their minds.

Majority influence

The assumption is that people usually like to fit in with a larger group. At the same time, the group itself exerts social pressure on people to conform to accepted ways of thinking and behaving. These are called social norms. Majority influence happens when people see or experience the 'norms' of a group and then adopt the same or similar values and behaviours.

To test if this is true, Solomon Asch, a US social psychologist, carried out some famous studies in the early 1950s (Asch, 1952). He invited groups of students to take part in vision tests where he asked them to call out the relative lengths of lines drawn on paper by their fellow students. Unknown to one student, all the others were collaborators and deliberately called out a false answer. The aim was to see if the innocent student would call out a wrong answer to fit in with group norms. Thirty-two per cent did so. This experiment has been much criticized for its methods and its conclusions, which seemed just to reflect the social norms of the United States at the time. One unexpected result was that if a minority view was expressed, resistance to conformity increased. This was picked up in later experiments by Serge Moscovici and colleagues (Moscovici, Lage and Naffrechoux, 1969).

Deutsch and Gerard subsequently suggested that people conform for two different reasons. Normative influence occurs when someone conforms in order to obtain approval from the group (Deutsch and Gerard, 1955). Informational influence occurs when an individual conforms because they are persuaded of the superior knowledge of others.

Kelman (1958) argued that there are three ways in which conformity is demonstrated:

1 Compliance – behaviour changes to gain the rewards of identifying with the group but the person's values are unchanged.

2 Identification – behaviour changes and the person appreciates conforming to the group.

3 Internalization – behaviour changes, as do the person's values and thinking.

Later research by Bond and Smith (1996) found that conformity is as much a response to a country's culture as an individual's preference.

Minority influence

This happens when a minority, even just one person, influences a majority to change their behaviour or views. Moscovici and others (Moscovici and Nemeth, 1974; Moscovici, 1985) set out some conditions for the majority to be influenced by the minority:

1 Consistency – the minority should be undivided and consistent in what they are saying.

2 Flexibility – the minority should appear to be reasonable people and not too confrontational or rigid.

3 Commitment – if the minority are clearly very committed to their position, this will challenge people to rethink their views.

4 Relevance – if the minority's views are in line with broader social trends, they are more likely to succeed.

It's also clear that minority influence takes place over a longer period of time and involves the idea of conversion. Conversion usually involves both public and private acceptance of a new view or behaviour. Given that majorities are generally unconcerned about what minorities think of them, change often happens when the minority provides new information that shifts opinions.

More recent studies by Van Avermaet have shown that engaging the leader of a majority group by someone from the minority who is consistent in their ideas and behaviour will have a positive influencing effect. Good leadership is key for a minority group to persuade others (Van Avermaet, 1996).

So what?

These ideas have a potentially wide range of applications within organizations and in the marketplace. Mannix and Neale (2005) argue that majorities tend towards convergent or one-track thinking, while the presence of minorities prompts much deeper and more divergent reflection on a topic. This adds value and improves the quality of decision making. De Dreu and others make clear connections between high levels of minority influence and high degrees of creativity and innovation within teams (De Dreu and West, 2001; Martin and Hewstone, 2009). A caveat is that, for this to work, there needs to be a high degree of participative decision making.

In the realms of marketing more attention is being paid to social media influencers. These are people who make extensive use of Facebook, Twitter and blogs to broadcast their opinions on products and services. Although a minority, they consistently, and over a period of time, communicate persuasive information. At first glance, such a person may appear independent but increasingly companies are recruiting and training social media influencers to advocate on their behalf (see, for example, **http://www.magnoninternational.com/**). Work has also been done in evaluating the relative effectiveness of advertising campaigns focused on minority and majority groups (Grier and Deshpandé, 2001).

More widely, minority influence has been felt in social trends ranging from the suffragette movement through to climate change awareness and the cessation of smoking in public places.

What else?

The studies by both Asch and Moscovici have been regularly criticized for being conducted in laboratory conditions and probably identify compliance rather than conformity. Cultural differences also have a strong bearing on how and when influence happens (Bond and Smith, 1996).

What everyone seems to agree upon is that social influence happens but, in reality, is a very complex set of processes.

Leadership challenge

When have you observed majority or minority influence at work in your team? What were the factors at play and what were the outcomes for the organization? How can you use these ideas to effect change?

More help

http://blog.magnoninternational.com/the-social-influence-marketing/

Key references

Asch, S E (1952) *Group Forces in the Modification and Distortion of Judgments*, Prentice-Hall, Englewood Cliffs, NJ

Moscovici, S, Lage, E and Naffrechoux, M (1969) Influence of a consistent minority on the responses of a majority in a color perception task, *Sociometry*, **37** (4), pp 529–40

Other references

Bond, R and Smith, P B (1996) Culture and conformity: a meta-analysis of studies using Asch's (1952b, 1956) line judgment task, *Psychological Bulletin*, **119** (1), pp 111–37

De Dreu, C K W and West, M A (2001) Minority dissent and team innovation: the importance of participation in decision making, *Journal of Applied Psychology*, **86** (6), pp 1191–1201

Deutsch, M and Gerard, H B (1955) A study of normative and informational social influences upon individual judgment, *Journal of Abnormal and Social Psychology*, **51** (3), pp 629–36

Grier, S A and Deshpandé, R (2001) Social dimensions of consumer distinctiveness: the influence of social status on group identity and advertising persuasion, *Journal of Marketing Research*, **38** (2), pp 216–24

Kelman, H C (1958) Compliance, identification, and internalization: three processes of attitude change, *Journal of Conflict Resolution*, **2** (1), pp 51–60

Mannix, E and Neale, M A (2005) What differences make a difference? *Psychological Science in the Public Interest*, **6** (2), pp 31–55

Martin, R and Hewstone, M (2009) *Minority Influence and Innovation: Antecedents, processes and consequences*, Psychology Press, Hove, Sussex

Moscovici, S (1985) Social influence and conformity, in *Handbook of Social Psychology*, vol. 2, eds G Lindzy and E Aronson, pp 347–412, Random House, New York

Moscovici, S and Nemeth, C (1974) Social influence: II. Minority influence, in *Social Psychology: Classic and contemporary integrations*, ed C. Nemeth, Social Psychology: Classic and contemporary integrations, Rand McNally, Chicago

Van Avermaet, E (1996) Social influence in small groups, in *Introduction to Social Psychology*, ed V M Hewstone, W Stroebe and G M Stephenson, pp 350–60, Blackwell, Oxford

How can we positively help people and teams change?

32

The Skilled Helper Model

The big idea

Gerard Egan, a US professor of psychology, first published his Skilled Helper Model in the 1970s (Egan, 1975). Its original focus was to support the practice of counsellors and therapists by providing what Egan now prefers to call a framework. This framework has two main functions. First, it sets out the territory of 'helping', and second, it identifies the types of task involved and how they interrelate. Subsequently, the framework has been adopted and adapted by change managers, trainers, educators and organizational development specialists who have found it useful in mapping and supporting large-scale development efforts. The framework doesn't prescribe what approaches individual helpers might wish to take at each point but does suggest stages through which the change process will go. Egan describes the framework as 'atheoretical' and integrated because it does not explicitly support a particular set of theories about change (Wosket, 2006). However, he does draw upon the work of the eminent psychologist Carl Rogers (Rogers, 1957) by assuming that the helper will practise Rogerian core helping qualities of empathy, genuineness and respect in any relationship. Active listening, which pays attention to the client's verbal and non-verbal communications, is also considered by Egan as an essential element of a dynamic helping relationship.

So what?

The framework is usually represented by a diagram like Figure 32.1.

FIGURE 32.1   The Skilled Helper framework

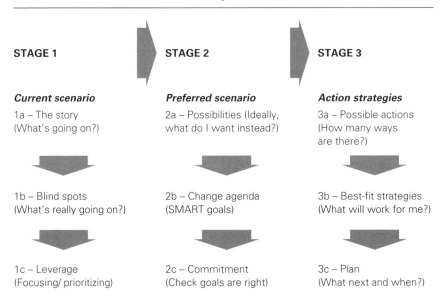

STAGE 1	STAGE 2	STAGE 3
Current scenario	*Preferred scenario*	*Action strategies*
1a – The story (What's going on?)	2a – Possibilities (Ideally, what do I want instead?)	3a – Possible actions (How many ways are there?)
1b – Blind spots (What's really going on?)	2b – Change agenda (SMART goals)	3b – Best-fit strategies (What will work for me?)
1c – Leverage (Focusing/ prioritizing)	2c – Commitment (Check goals are right)	3c – Plan (What next and when?)

Action leading to valued outcomes

In a nutshell, the framework aims to help a client answer three main questions:

1 What is happening?

2 What do I want to happen instead?

3 How might I get to what I want?

Not everyone will necessarily need to answer all three and the process of helping may involve moving backwards and forwards between each stage. Egan says this is to be expected.

The process

Stage 1 Current scenario

The starting point is the client's story about what is happening to them. The helper uses open questions to encourage them to explore all dimensions of the story and to begin to see aspects of it which they may not have noticed before. The client is asked where they wish to focus their energies.

Stage 2 Preferred scenario

There can be a tendency for people to move straight from problem to action. This second stage asks them to stop and think what they really want. In this way, the problem might come to be seen as an opportunity rather than a hindrance. The potential is for hope to be generated in the client's thinking.

Stage 3 Action strategies

The final stage is helping the client clarify actions they can take to move towards their desired goals. The helper offers opportunities to brainstorm ideas and plans. The challenge to the client at the end is to be as specific as possible about when and how they will take their next steps.

Those who use this framework speak of a dynamic energy in the process that enables people to move from one stage through another and back to the beginning. It's a versatile and flexible framework that takes account of a wide variety of contexts. As the narrative at the start unfolds, so what needs to happen becomes more apparent and the finally agreed action is often quite different from that which was originally envisaged.

Feltham and Horton (2006) suggest that 'at its best it is a shared map that helps clients participate more fully in the helping process'. Egan, in his later work, emphasizes client empowerment and adopts a positive psychology perspective. He says that the two principal goals of the framework are to: 1) help clients manage their problems in living more effectively and develop unused resources and missed opportunities fully; and 2) help clients become better at helping themselves in their everyday lives (Egan, 2002).

The role of the helper is to facilitate the client to work with the freedom they have in their circumstances to take the action they want to take. Minimum intervention is a principle of how in practice the framework is intended to be applied.

What else?

Because Egan does not prescribe particular approaches to personal change, few people have criticized the framework. The general view is that it is an intuitively helpful outline which supports counsellors and change facilitators think through steps they can use in their practice. The framework has its theoretical origins in a range of other learning and change theories, including Carkhuff's, Strong's, and Bandura's (Bandura, 1977; Carkhuff, 1971; Strong, 1968). There is also a suggestion that it owes many of its ideas to Ignatian approaches to spiritual direction (Russon, 2003).

Leadership challenge

Invite two colleagues to join you to use the framework to practise coaching conversations using live issues. One person acts as an observer and feeds back at the end what they notice about how the framework adds value to the process.

More help

Key reference

Egan, G (2009) *The Skilled Helper: A problem-management and opportunity-development approach to helping*, Brooks/Cole, Pacific Grove, CA

Other references

Bandura, A (1977) Self-efficacy: toward a unifying theory of behavioral change, *Psychological Review*, **84** (2), pp 191–215

Carkhuff, R R (1971) Training as a preferred mode of treatment, *Journal of Counseling Psychology*, **18** (2), pp 123–31

Egan, G (1975) *The Skilled Helper: A model for systematic helping and inter-personal relating*, Brooks/Cole, Monterey, CA

Egan, G (2002) *The Skilled Helper*, Brooks/Cole, Pacific Grove, CA

Feltham, C and Horton, I (2006) *The SAGE Handbook of Counselling and Psychotherapy*, Sage, Thousand Oaks, CA

Rogers, C R (1957) The necessary and sufficient conditions of therapeutic personality change, *Journal of Consulting Psychology*, **21** (2), pp 95–103

Russon, M (2003) A 'common sense' approach to reflection, Education-line, University of Leeds, UK

Strong, S R (1968) Counseling: an interpersonal influence process, *Journal of Counseling Psychology*, **15** (3), pp 215–24

Wosket, V (2006) The Skilled Helper Model, in *The SAGE Handbook of Counselling and Psychotherapy*, ed C Feltham and I Horton, Sage, Thousand Oaks, CA

33

How does shift work impact on how well people do their work?

Circadian rhythms and performance at work

The big idea

Circadian rhythms are natural human physiological processes that follow a roughly 24-hour cycle (Halberg *et al*, 1959). These processes include sleep–wake cycles, body temperature, blood pressure and the release of hormones. The Latin term *circa* means 'around' and *dian* or *diem* means 'day'. Similar rhythms have been observed in other animals as well as plants. The rhythms are routines built into our bodies but adjusted and affected by external factors (called 'zeitgebers'), such as daylight.

People can be categorized along a continuum of chronotypes (Roenneberg, Wirz-Justice and Merrow, 2003). 'Morning people', often known as larks, like to go to bed early and wake around sunrise. Night people, often known as owls, prefer to sleep longer in the morning and go to bed later. If people get the sleep they need to function well and can adjust their timings when they need to, then both are normal circadian rhythms.

To keep rhythms steady there have to be regular time cues or zeitgebers such as sunrise, sunset and a daily routine. When people experience an inability to match their sleep–wake cycle with the environmental cues, they are likely to be unable to sleep and wake up at regular times. The most common examples of this are jet lag and shift-work sleep disorder. Some people have waking or sleeping problems because of medical conditions unrelated to any external cues.

So what?

Research in recent years has focused on the impact of disrupted circadian rhythms on shift workers and professional staff such as medical and nursing staff who undertake night duties on a regular basis (Barger *et al*, 2006; Åkerstedt, 2003). Sleep, or the disruption of it, has been blamed for significant human errors that have led to air crashes and other catastrophes. In a hospital context, night shift-work patterns are said to contribute to increased rates of patient safety incidents (Coffey, Skipper Jr and Jung, 1988). The main concern is the impact of disruption on workers who sometimes work at night and sometimes during the day. It is perhaps unsurprising that research confirms that the quality of task performance tends to mirror the circadian sleep–wake cycle. Desynchronization of the rhythms by shift-work patterns leads to decreases in work efficiency and makes workers more susceptible to making errors (Åkerstedt, 2003).

People's reactions to disrupted rhythms vary. Some feel a constant sense of tiredness and disorientation. Other may have uncontrollable urges to sleep, stomach problems and the inability to focus on a task. Research suggests that people whose rhythms are regularly disrupted over an extended period of time can have a greater susceptibility to cancer, gastrointestinal and cardiovascular disorders. Some of these may also be related to the lifestyle factors associated with shift work, such as eating poor-quality food at irregular times (Canadian Centre for Occupational Health and Safety, 2010).

There are a number of practical steps businesses can take to help shift workers remain safe and effective in their jobs:

- Optimize the design of the shift schedule so that it balances personal, psychological, social and medical concerns. There is continuing debate about the benefits of either a seven-day rotation period or a rapid rotation where different shifts are worked every two or three days. Research, however, agrees that a forward rotation seems preferable, involving a move of the pattern of shifts from morning to afternoon to night. Circadian rhythms adjust better when moving forward (Muecke, 2005).

- Build in 24-hour rest times between a change in shift patterns and avoid shifts starting early in the morning or very late at night.

- Provide time off when workers can socialize with their families and ensure that shifts are notified well in advance to help everyone plan their social lives.

- Ensure proper rest facilities and nourishing food for night workers. This maintains motivation and healthy eating.

- Educate staff on how to manage the stresses of shift work.

Individuals can look after themselves by:

- eating regularly and well at set times;
- setting aside specific times for sleep;
- sleeping in a room that is dark, comfortable and with the phone disconnected;
- learning and practising relaxation techniques;
- keeping physically fit and making time for leisure and social activities.

What else?

There is consensus that circadian rhythms impact on the ability of shift workers to adjust to new patterns of working. However, there is disagreement about the extent to which individuals may be affected. The impact of shift work is greater on some people than on others. Research suggests that workers above the age of 40 are less able to manage the change in sleep–wake patterns that shift work entails (Coffey *et al*, 1988).

Of interest to staff trainers and group facilitators is the observation that the post-lunch attention dip in training sessions is an important factor to consider. It is generally agreed that this results from participants digesting food consumed at lunch, although more important is the body-rhythm–body-temperature dip which takes place in the early afternoon (Shiftworker Online, 2011).

Leadership challenges

How do you think working patterns affect the performance of your team? What adjustments can you make to improve well-being and effectiveness?

More help

Key references

Canadian Centre for Occupational Health and Safety (9 November 2010 [accessed 8 September 2011]) *Shiftwork* [Online] http://www.ccohs.ca/oshanswers/ergonomics/shiftwrk.html
Shiftworker Online [accessed 8 September 2011] Circadian rhythm room, http://shiftworker.tripod.com/crhythm.html

Other references

Åkerstedt, T (2003) Shift work and disturbed sleep/wakefulness, *Occupational Medicine*, **53** (2), pp 89–94

Barger, L K, Ayas, N T, Cade, B E *et al* (2006) Impact of extended-duration shifts on medical errors, adverse events, and attentional failures, *PLoS Medicine*, **3** (12), p e487

Coffey, L C, Skipper Jr, J K and Jung, F D (1988) Nurses and shift work: effects on job performance and job-related stress, *Journal of Advanced Nursing*, **13** (2), pp 245–54

Halberg, F, Halberg, E, Barnum, C *et al* (1959) Physiologic 24-hour periodicity in human beings and mice, the lighting regimen and daily routine, in *Photoperiodism and Related Phenomena in Plants and Animals*, ed R B Withrow, pp 803–78, American Association for the Advancement of Science, Washington, DC

Muecke, S (2005) Effects of rotating night shifts: literature review, *Journal of Advanced Nursing*, **50** (4), pp 433–9

Roenneberg, T, Wirz-Justice, A and Merrow, M (2003) Life between clocks: daily temporal patterns of human chronotypes, *Journal of Biological Rhythms*, **18** (1), pp 80–90

How do groups develop to become effective?

34

Tuckman's group development

The big idea

Bruce Tuckman's 'Forming, Storming, Norming, Performing and Adjourning' concept is probably the most well known amongst the many theories about how groups work. It's frequently used by facilitators to help groups understand how they can become more effective. With its snappy phrasing and simple linear form it is easy to understand why its popularity has grown since Tuckman first published it in 1965 (Tuckman, 1965). The final 'Adjourning' or ending stage was added by Tuckman and his colleague Mary Ann Jensen after a review of the theory in the mid-1970s (Tuckman and Jensen, 1977). See Figure 34.1.

To come up with the theory Tuckman reviewed academic research and theory papers. From these he identified that all groups initially appear to have four sequential development stages in common. These are:

- *Forming*. Groups start by orientating themselves to establish who they are and what they are intended to achieve. This is accompanied by people testing boundaries and developing relationships among themselves and with leaders in the group.

- *Storming*. Resistance becomes apparent as conflict about roles and relationships occurs. Emotional responses from group members can create tension within interpersonal relationships.

- *Norming*. Initial resistance is overcome by the adoption of new standards and roles that create a unique group culture. Members feel a sense of togetherness in the task and among each other, with a new freedom to express personal opinions.

- *Performing*. This stage is characterized by interdependence between group members as they focus on performing the task.

FIGURE 34.1 Tuckman's model (adapted)

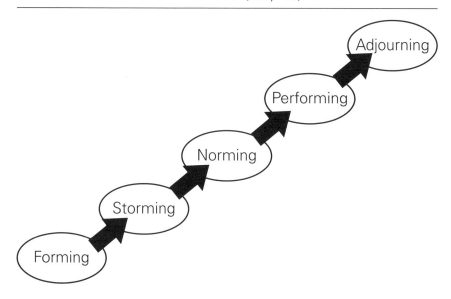

Tuckman and Jensen's fifth stage is:

- *Adjourning*. At this point the group task comes to an end and people return to their roles as individuals. There may be a degree of sadness among group members, so some people call this the 'mourning' stage.

So what?

The theory opens up more questions for groups as they develop than perhaps it answers. For example, no clues are given by Tuckman about the length of time an effective group should stay in each phase. Nor are there any ideas about what triggers a shift from one phase to the next. That said, some writers suggest that the theory offers a good predictor about what will happen as a group is formed (Hellriegel, Slocum Jr and Woodman, 1992).

There are some bigger questions asked by psychologists who wonder if group development can really be described in such a linear way. Groups and individuals tend to deviate from developing in predictable ways, so there are bound to be overlaps between stages and a degree of ambiguity about what happens when. Furthermore, stages may be missed altogether or repeated as a result of factors such as prior relationships, personality traits of members and the nature of the task.

In real life, it's argued, people don't spend much time thinking about process. They generally leap in and get on with the task. A pattern for how they develop thus emerges as they get on with the task and encounter hurdles along the way. Tasks also differ in scale and type, and this will also have an impact on how a group works (Herriot and Pemberton, 1995). Further, in today's business environment people are often members of many groups at the same time and this may well add a further level of complexity to inter-relationships and group development needs.

Other theorists have proposed that a cyclical model is more accurate, arguing, for example, that group members move between trying to accomplish a task and building relationships within the group (Hare, Borgatta and Bales, 1965).

What else?

In spite of all the criticism of the theory it remains popular with facilitators and groups who tend to identify with the stages even if their own experience differs in practice. There is a danger that facilitators may label groups as having reached particular stages and treat them accordingly. An alternative is to use the theory as a metaphor and a self-assessment tool to prompt reflection. Managers of teams similarly find it a helpful way of understanding what types of intervention may be useful as they seek to support a group in becoming more effective. In the early stages a directive approach will focus the group on what it needs to accomplish. Once norms have been established and the group performs, the model suggests that less external direction is required.

Leadership challenge

Ask your team to reflect on their own experience of the group and how it matches or differs from the Tuckman theory.

More help

Key references

Tuckman, B W (1965) Developmental sequence in small groups, *Psychological Bulletin*, **63** (6), pp 384–99

Tuckman, B W and Jensen, M A C (1977) Stages of small-group development revisited, *Group and Organization Management*, **2** (4), pp 419–27

Other references

Hare, A P, Borgatta, E F and Bales, R F (eds) (1965) *Small Groups: Studies in social interaction*, Knopf, New York

Hellriegel, D, Slocum Jr, J and Woodman, R (1992) *Organizational Behaviour*, 6th edn, West Publishing, St Paul, MN

Herriot, P and Pemberton, C (1995) *Competitive Advantage through Diversity: Organizational learning from difference*, Sage, Thousand Oaks, CA

How can you ensure everyone makes a fair contribution to team goals?

35

Social loafing theory

The big idea

Social loafing happens when individuals put less effort into group work than when they work on their own. It was first written about by a French engineer, Max Ringelmann, who noticed that individuals in a tug-of-war competition expended less individual effort as more people joined in the activity. This is known as the Ringelmann effect (Ringelmann, 1913). Since then, much research has been done to better understand this phenomenon and to find ways of reducing social loafing. Latané, Williams and Harkins (1979), who coined the term social loafing, confirm that Ringelmann's observations are not just about poor coordination, which sometimes happens in groups, but is definitely the result of reduced individual effort. They conclude that increasing the size of the group means that relative social pressure on individuals to perform reduces. When this is combined with a lack of identifiable rewards for individual performance, people are likely to work less hard. Developing this theme, Karau and Williams propose a collective effort model (CEM) (Karau and Williams, 1993). Their idea is that the motivation to work well in a group depends on having your self-belief that you can do the task, that it will make a difference and that you will be recognized by others for your contribution. They also found that people will loaf more when:

- it's difficult to evaluate personal contributions;
- the task seems meaningless;

- group size is large;
- the culture is more individualistic and less collectivistic;
- tasks are complex;
- individuals expect other group members to be better contributors;
- the group lacks cohesion and is unlikely to be compared with the performance of other similar groups.

In a nutshell, people work harder when they can see a connection between their individual effort and personal rewards.

Chidambaram and Tung confirm that group size is particularly important when it comes to performance of a task. A smaller group (fewer than 10 members) will perform better than a larger one. If group members work in the same office, there also tends to be social pressure to appear to be working harder than if people work alone (Chidambaram and Tung, 2005).

A parallel phenomenon is the 'sucker' effect. People often think that others in a group will leave them to get on with all the work while the group ends up taking the credit instead of them. As a result, people reduce the amount of effort they put in to avoid feeling a fool. For example, where there is an absence culture at work, people can assume they have the right to take a number of days' sick leave even if they are well. Someone who chooses not to take this leave may feel that they carry an unfair share of the work. They perceive themselves to be a 'sucker'! The consequence, confirmed by Harkins and Jackson, is that people will reduce their efforts to match the performance of those who are slacking (Harkins and Jackson, 1985).

So what?

There are plenty of practical approaches that will reduce social loafing and enhance group performance. Rothwell suggests three Cs to get a group to perform well:

1 *Collaboration* – assign every group member a specific meaningful task.
2 *Content* – ensure that every individual's task explicitly connects with the achievement of the group's objective.
3 *Choice* – give group members choices about which task they want to do. This strengthens personal ownership and encourages people to work together as a group.

(Rothwell, 1999)

Thompson says that a group needs to coordinate itself well, ensuring it effectively uses all the skills of its members. There are two groups of strategies that will achieve this, those that build motivation and those that enhance coordination:

Motivation strategies:

- increase the identifiability of individual contributions;
- promote involvement;
- reward group members for performance;
- strengthen group cohesion;
- increase personal responsibility;
- develop contracts with a group;
- provide group performance reviews and feedback.

Coordination strategies:

- restrict the size of groups to under 10 members;
- have a clear agenda;
- train group members together;
- spend more time practising tasks;
- minimize links in the communication chain;
- set clear shared performance standards.

(Adapted from Thompson, 2000)

There are complementary ideas from other writers, including the need to select group members carefully, set ground rules, routinely evaluate progress, encourage socializing between members and celebrate success at regular intervals. When creatively combined, social loafing by individuals can be reduced.

If there is a social loafer in a group, Rothwell suggests a range of strategies that may help improve their contribution, including one-to-one confrontation, group discussion, involving the boss, getting round them by reallocating tasks and, as a last resort, excluding them from the group (Rothwell, 1999).

What else?

It's worth bearing in mind that social loafing doesn't always happen. There is some research that indicates that people may work harder in a group when they perceive that their fellow group members are of lower ability than they are (Karau and Williams, 1997). The differences in cultural backgrounds of group members and their impact on performance are well documented. Those from an Eastern culture are likely to see the performance of the group as more important than how they are perceived as an individual (Earley, 1989). Research also suggests that women are more inclined to consider group cohesion as a priority when compared to men, who will tend to focus on task achievement. As a result, women, it is argued, are less likely to engage in social loafing (Kugihara, 1999).

Leadership challenge

Ask your team whether the theory is true from their own experience. If so, how can social loafing be tackled?

More help

Key references

Karau, S J and Williams, K D (1993) Social loafing: a meta-analytic review and theoretical integration, *Journal of Personality and Social Psychology*, **65** (4), pp 681–706

Rothwell, J D (1999) *In the Company of Others: An introduction to communication*, Mayfield, Mountain View, CA

Other references

Chidambaram, L and Tung, L L (2005) Is out of sight, out of mind? An empirical study of social loafing in technology-supported groups, *Information Systems Research*, **16** (2), pp 149–68

Earley, P C (1989) Social loafing and collectivism: a comparison of the United States and the People's Republic of China, *Administrative Science Quarterly*, **34**, pp 565–81

Harkins, S G and Jackson, J M (1985) The role of evaluation in eliminating social loafing, *Personality and Social Psychology Bulletin*, **11** (4), pp 457–65

Karau, S J and Williams, K D (1997) The effects of group cohesiveness on social loafing and social compensation, *Group Dynamics: Theory, Research, and Practice*, **1** (2), pp 156–68

Kugihara, N (1999) Gender and social loafing in Japan, *The Journal of Social Psychology*, **139** (4), pp 516–26

Latané, B, Williams, K and Harkins, S (1979) Many hands make light the work: the causes and consequences of social loafing, *Journal of Personality and Social Psychology*, **37** (6), pp 822–32

Ringelmann, M (1913) Research on animate sources of power: the work of man, *Annales De l'Instuit National Agronomique*, **12**, pp 1–40

Thompson, L L (2000) *Making the team: A guide for managers*, Prentice-Hall, Upper Saddle River, NJ

How do you get good outcomes for both sides in a negotiation?

36

Best alternative to a negotiated agreement (BATNA)

The big idea

Getting to Yes is a hugely popular book on negotiation strategy by Harvard academics Roger Fisher and William Ury (Fisher and Ury, 1981). Since it was first published in 1981 it has been consistently at the top of the best-seller lists. Such has been its impact that some say it prompted a 'big bang' in the evolution of business negotiation theory and practice (Thompson and Leonardelli, 2004).

At the heart of the theory is the belief that wise agreements help develop positive relationships between people. The traditional approach to bargaining has had both parties set out their demands and then make moves to come closer together. Ultimately they get to an agreed deal. The authors argue that this is not a very efficient way of negotiating, nor does it build good relationships which are vital if a deal is going to be implemented smoothly. Such positional negotiating was, for example, characteristic of industrial relations in the UK during the 1970s and 1980s. Deals were eventually done between employers and trade unions but the resulting relationships were so poor that modernization plans, needing a spirit of positive coopera-tion, often failed to materialize. This cycle is of no ultimate benefit to either side. To overcome this pattern Fisher and Ury propose that old-style positional negotiation be replaced by principled negotiation. This has four key elements which:

1 separate the people from the problem;
2 focus on interests rather than positions;
3 generate a variety of options before settling on an agreement;
4 insist that the agreement be based on objective criteria.

(Adapted from Fisher and Ury, 1981)

The first principle recognizes the emotions involved when people negotiate. These, when combined with communication challenges, can make negotiating a very fraught experience. Focusing on the problem rather than seeing everything as a personal attack helps make progress. The second principle encourages negotiators to consider carefully the ultimate goal of the process for both parties, rather than just the various positions each takes during its course. The third principle suggests that creative thinking and a wide-ranging joint exploration of possible options speed up reaching a constructive agreement. The final principle proposes the use of objective criteria to act as a reference point for both parties during negotiations.

What for many is the most useful aspect of the *Getting to Yes* approach is the idea that the weaker party should concentrate on developing their best alternative to a negotiated agreement (BATNA). If you are that weaker party, it's a way of both protecting yourself from an unwise agreement and making the most of your assets and options. A good BATNA will give you more power in a negotiation. The required steps to develop a BATNA are:

1 inventing a list of actions you might conceivably take if no agreement can be reached;
2 improving some of the more promising ideas and converting them into practical alternatives;
3 selecting, tentatively, the one option that seems best.

(Fisher, Ury and Patton, 1992)

Once completed, the weaker party has a tool that helps it reject possible agreements that may be less advantageous than their BATNA. The whole idea of negotiating is, after all, to produce better outcomes than can be achieved by other means. The BATNA differs from the 'bottom line', which is usually a fixed financial sum representing the point below which a party will cease negotiations.

So what?

Given the importance of managing the power and psychological dynamics in a negotiation, BATNA can help the weaker (or weakened) negotiator by:

1 Clarifying the range of alternatives to be included as part of a final deal. This builds confidence and helps both parties move away from 'either/or' positions.

2 Helping them see aspects of a proposal that may be helpful to achieving their final desired outcome rather than discarding them prematurely.

3 Avoiding the psychological aggregation of alternatives. People often assume that they may have many choices if a negotiation fails when in reality they will have to choose between one or another option. The sum total of all choices is not possible!

4 Preventing the stress people feel when they contemplate the possible failure of negotiations. This can make them too willing to compromise just to finish the process.

5 Encouraging the formulation of what Fisher *et al* call a 'trip wire'. This is an agreement that is far from perfect but will give early warning if something unacceptable is about to be put on the table.

6 Enhancing the attractiveness of *not* reaching agreement. This creates a sense of power and control over the process and outcomes.

7 Helping the negotiator see that if negotiations do fail, there are other options.

8 By considering the other side's possible BATNA, negotiating approaches can be more carefully prepared for.

9 Encouraging all parties to focus on the merits of an argument.

If both parties have a strong BATNA there may be no need to proceed with the negotiation at all!

What else?

Research on negotiation strategies is still unable to help predict the likely result of a specific negotiation (Van Poucke and Buelens, 2002). There is also a view that the focus on interests rather than positions as popularized by *Getting to Yes* can be counterproductive. This is because negotiations can hinge on people's values and perceptions in a way that prompts them to focus on key positions, rather than broader interests, as a way of being heard (Provis, 1996). Majoring on interests can also be open to manipulation and deception by either party, where one side only pretends to be friendly. The negotiation will break down when this becomes obvious, as one side then suddenly takes a hard position (Senger, 2002).

External forces also play a major factor in the progress of negotiations, as do cultural contexts. DuBrin (2002), for example, gives detailed guidance on the attitudinal and behavioural challenges facing a US negotiator in a Chinese or Arabic environment.

Leadership challenge

Ask your team to prepare a BATNA for a negotiation they are facing in the near future. Review how helpful this was at the end of the negotiation process.

More help

Key reference

Fisher, R and Ury, W (1981) *Getting to Yes*, Houghton Mifflin, Boston

Other references

DuBrin, A J (2002) *Fundamentals of Organizational Behavior*, Thomson Learning, Mason, OH

Fisher, R, Ury, W L and Patton, B (1992) Original explanation of BATNA, in *Getting to Yes: Negotiating agreement without giving in*, 2nd edn, pp 101–11, Houghton Mifflin, Boston

Provis, C (1996) Interests vs positions: a critique of the distinction, *Negotiation Journal*, **12** (4), pp 305–23

Senger, J M (2002) Tales of the bazaar: interest-based negotiation across cultures, *Negotiation Journal*, **18** (3), pp 233–50

Thompson, L and Leonardelli, G J (2004) The big bang: the evolution of negotiation research, *The Academy of Management Executive*, **18** (3), pp 113–17

Van Poucke, D and Buelens, M (2002) Predicting the outcome of a two-party price negotiation: contribution of reservation price, aspiration price and opening offer, *Journal of Economic Psychology*, **23** (1), pp 67–76

37

How do I make decisions in a complex world?

Cynefin complexity model

The big idea

The Cynefin model is a framework which has been developed to help leaders make decisions in dynamic changing environments. The framework was developed by Dr Dave Snowden during his time at IBM, and now forms part of his work at his independent consulting company, Cognitive Edge. The framework was popularized by an article in *Harvard Business Review* (Snowden and Boon, 2007).

Cynefin is a Welsh word, which is commonly translated into English as 'habitat', although this fails to describe the meaning fully. A more complete translation of the word would be that it is a special place where multiple pasts reflected in our faith, cultural heritage and belonging come together. The term was chosen to illustrate the evolutionary nature of complex systems, including their inherent uncertainty. The name is a reminder that all human interactions and how we make sense of them are strongly influenced and frequently determined by our experiences.

The model provides a typology of contexts that guides what sort of explanations or solutions may apply in a range of situations facing modern leaders. The model draws on research into complex theory, cognitive science and narrative patterns.

The framework, which has most often been presented as a decision-making heuristic, has multiple uses and tools. These are summarized on the Cognitive Edge website – **www.cognitive-edge.com**.

The model (see Figure 37.1) suggests that most managers in organizations see problems as containing a high degree of order and predictability.

FIGURE 37.1   Complexity framework

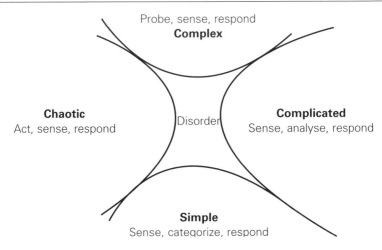

SOURCE: Snowden and Boone (2007)

This assumption is grounded in Newtonian science – the relationship between cause and effect. Snowden casts these types of problem as either simple or complicated. For simple problems managers believe that they can identify a solution; for complicated problems they draw on expert advice or guidance from professional accountants, auditors or external consultants. However, Snowden suggests that the simple–complicated division is a false view of the world. Both assume that there is a direct relationship between cause and effect; that is, an intervention of X leads to a planned and predictable outcome of Y. In the former case the skills of the manager are often adequate to identify a solution. In the latter, expert help is required. This is not to say that problems cannot arise, for example in classifying the problem incorrectly, or in implementing the solution. However, in general, the solutions for simple and complicated problems are often more easily within grasp. In simple cases the individual or organization can follow a three-step process: the 'sense, categorize and respond' approach to problems. This involves gathering data, using this data to categorize the problem and then acting to resolve the problem based on the data. For problems categorized as 'complicated', the manager will 'sense, analyse and respond'. The change from categorize to analyse reflects the need for greater thinking as a result of more, or more complicated, data.

Snowden argues that in a modern, connected and multiple-stakeholder world, complexity exists. In this world the relationship between cause and effect is less direct. Outcomes can be unpredictable or, at best, are difficult to see fully.

In the first of these, managers need to undertake a three-stage process involving 'probe, sense and respond'. The 'complex' space means that the relationship between cause and effect may only make sense with 'retrospective coherence' – as we look back on events. The manager thus tests interventions out through pilot schemes and other small projects and gathers some data on their initial impact. If the feeling is that the impact is positive, more is invested in this intervention, with effort being shifted from things that don't work to those that do, gradually over time. A plan thus emerges for what actions the manager takes, based on feedback from the system itself.

The final space is that of 'chaos'. In chaos there is no relationship between cause and effect, partly due to the multiple players and their interactions, meaning that similar interventions will not create the same response twice – as outcomes will depend on content, situation and the multiple stakeholders interacting creating the system outcome. In these situations the manager needs to try to impose order on the system through action, while lightly gathering data and making a judgement about a final response.

Unlike other four-box models the framework offers a fifth space – 'Disorder'. The very nature of the fifth space makes it particularly difficult to recognize when one is in it. In this space multiple perspectives jostle for prominence, factional leaders argue with one another and cacophony rules. The way out of this realm is to break down the situation into constituent parts and assign each to one of the other four realms. Leaders can then make decisions and intervene.

So what?

The framework has been taken up by governments as well as commercial organizations seeking to operate in multiple markets with multiple stakeholders. Singapore, for example, applied the framework in responding to the SARS (severe acute respiratory syndrome) virus, while the US Defense Advanced Research Projects Agency has applied the framework to its work with counterterrorism (Snowden and Boon, 2007).

For organizational managers grappling with managing change in complex environments or thinking about marketing strategies and product launches, the model provides a fresh way to think about decisions and tools to plan possible scenarios and how the organization and its leadership might respond.

The framework has value for those making decisions as leaders, as well as consultants, working at national or organizational level, helping them to think through the nature of the problem they face and how best to intervene.

What else?

One of the weaknesses of the model is the need for individuals to be correctly able to categorize the problem into one of the four spaces. A failure to do so results in the problem being placed in disorder in order for the problem to be further broken down.

A second issue is managers' response to systemic thinking and complexity, as these frameworks move away from much of management thinking that has dominated the past hundred years. This paradigm assumes that problems can be analysed and solved through sufficient data collection, pattern identification or analysis.

Leadership challenge

Think about your largest challenge at work. Try to categorize the problem. Second, using the Cynefin model, develop an appropriate plan based on the three stages relevant to the category you have identified (be careful that many problems look like complicated ones but are in reality complex or even chaotic).

More help

Key reference

Snowden, D and Boon, M E (2007) A leader's framework for decision making, *Harvard Business Review*, November, pp 69–76

Other references

IBM Global Services (2001) *Sowing the Seeds of Organic Knowledge Management at English Nature*, IBM, Winchester

Snowden, D (2011) Stories from the frontier, *E-CO*, 8 (1), pp 85–8

How can we specify the behaviours required to perform a task well?

38

Critical incident technique

The big idea

In 1954 Colonel John C Flanagan, a psychologist working for the US Air Force, published a behavioural research method he called the critical incident technique (CIT).

He defined it as:

> a set of procedures for collecting direct observations of human behavior in such a way as to facilitate their potential usefulness in solving practical problems and developing broad psychological principles. The critical incident technique outlines procedures for collecting observed incidents having special significance and meeting systematically defined criteria.
>
> (Flanagan, 1954)

In practice, this involves researchers collecting brief written reports (or interview transcripts) from people who were either directly or indirectly involved in a critical incident. 'Critical' is an action that either improved a situation or led to a poorer than expected outcome. Researchers can also collect and use any relevant quantitative data. There are no restrictions on the type of data that can be included so long as they meet the criteria for reliability and validity established by the researchers at the outset.

So, for example, if a customer of a fast-food restaurant makes a serious complaint about poor service, a CIT process can include interviews with the customer, directly involved staff and customer feedback data. Staff on duty at the time could be asked to write short reports and if a CCTV camera happened to be facing the service counter, researchers might choose to analyse those images.

Flanagan makes the point that CIT should be considered a flexible set of principles that can be adapted to meet each situation. The focus of CIT is always to record and analyse how people actually behave in a specific situation. The aim is to identify the critical behavioural requirements for jobs that enable people to understand how a particular type of behaviour leads to a favourable outcome.

So what?

Flanagan suggests that five key steps are needed to complete a CIT process:

1 Determine the general aim of the activity.
2 Develop plans and specifications for collecting factual incidents regarding the activity.
3 Collect the data (either through interview or written up by the observer).
4 Analyse as objectively as possible.
5 Interpret and report on the requirements, particularly those which make a significant contribution to the activity.

(Adapted from Urquhart *et al*, 2003)

In a little more detail CIT steps involve the processes shown in Table 38.1.

CIT has been used in a work context for a wide range of purposes, including:

- measuring typical performance in a job role;
- establishing proficiency benchmarks for a task;
- training;
- job design;
- developing operating procedures;
- equipment design and ergonomics;
- motivation and leadership;
- skill development in coaching, counselling and psychotherapy;
- setting standards for recruitment and promotion.

Given the almost routine inclusion of defined behaviours as part of job and person specifications, HR professionals tend to be the primary users of CIT processes. This is particularly the case for activities and roles in organizations requiring high levels of technical competence combined with specific behaviours. Examples include surgeons, physicians, nurses, airline pilots, army personnel, educators and customer service staff (Serrat, 2010).

TABLE 38.1 CIT steps in detail

Critical incident step	Process
1. Identifying general aims	Describing a specific activity and what it is intended to achieve. This is the functional description. Researchers meet with people engaged in the activity to build a consensus around a description. A brief agreed statement is the output of this step.
2. Developing plans and specifications	Creating specific detailed rules for observers about what they are going to focus on and how their observations relate to the activity identified in the first step. Procedures need to help maintain as much objectivity as possible on the part of the observers. Prior to the next steps, training for observers is important.
3. Collecting the data	Data recording, evaluating and classification happen as close to the time of any incident as possible. Capturing specific and detailed observations of behaviours is important. Interviewing individuals or groups, using questionnaires and recording forms, are all options.
4. Analysing the data	Balancing the need to reduce the volume of material while retaining specificity is the challenge of this step.
5. Interpreting and reporting	Researchers honestly reflect in their final report the challenges they experience interpreting the data. Attempts are made to weigh the significance and relevance of the findings.

SOURCE: adapted from Flanagan (1954)

What else?

Research on CIT suggests that, when done well, it is a reliable process that also offers comparative value for money. It acknowledges that CIT can be resource intensive and requires investment in quality training for researchers to ensure that they adhere to the detailed procedural and interpretative aspects of the process (Koch *et al*, 2009; Ronan and Latham, 1974). Such training is vital if the focus of the process is not to shift entirely onto more extreme behaviours which are easier to observe and interpret. Capturing less obvious behaviours is equally important (Gremler, 2004). A risk with CIT is that the wider organizational factors affecting both the selection of incidents and their associated narratives are missed. This is why researchers will find it prudent to incorporate as wide a range of source data as is practicable. Too narrow a set of observations will introduce unhelpful bias (Serrat, 2010).

Leadership challenge

Ask your team to undertake a CIT process on a recent incident. What did you and they learn from this process?

More help

Key reference

Flanagan, J C (1954) The critical incident technique, *Psychological Bulletin*, **51** (4), pp 327–58

Other references

Gremler, D D (2004) The critical incident technique in service research, *Journal of Service Research*, **7** (1), pp 65–89

Koch, A, Strobel, A, Kici, G *et al* (2009) Quality of the critical incident technique in practice: interrater reliability and users' acceptance under real conditions, *Psychology Science Quarterly*, **51**, pp 3–15

Ronan, W W and Latham, G P (1974) The reliability and validity of the critical incident technique: a closer look, *Studies in Personnel Psychology*, **6**, pp 53–64

Serrat, O (2010) The critical incident, *Knowledge Solutions*, May, p 86

Urquhart, C, Light, A, Thomas, R *et al* (2003) Critical incident technique and explicitation interviewing in studies of information behavior, *Library and Information Science Research*, **25** (1), pp 63–88

PART THREE
Organizations

Creating and sustaining positive organizations

Working in organizations

Most of us will spend at least some time working as employees in organizations. The experience can be great, or something you prefer to try to forget. Either way there are insights from business psychology that can help us as individuals try to make the relationship a positive one. On the other side of the coin, there are ideas and models in this third part of the book that will help leaders of organizations create the right sort of environment for employees to flourish. We have included ideas about how to reduce stress, manage expectations and make the organization a fair place to work. The aim has to be to enable employees to make an excellent contribution to organizational goals while offering great relationships and high levels of job satisfaction.

Leading organizations through change

If leaders are going to add value it will be at times of organizational change. So it's critical that they are equipped with the mindsets, knowledge and behaviour that help them fulfil their responsibilities. We have taken a positive perspective by including approaches that respect the complexity of change and offer proven ways to maximize engagement, create energy and rapid progress. As realists we recognize that things don't always go smoothly, so we have incorporated ideas that help when resistance and difficult behaviours become apparent.

Learning to lead

We've not forgotten that becoming an effective leader is a lifelong learning process and so we have included some ideas that challenge the way we understand learning, leadership styles and the nature of organizations. They offer perspectives that take us out of our comfort zones and help us rethink what it means to demonstrate powerful leadership in our context.

Leadership challenge

Does anyone understand anything you write? It's a challenge for us as authors but in the age of e-mails, tweets and blogging, report writing is still a leadership challenge. Our last model in this book is slightly tongue in cheek but makes a serious point about the need for leaders to communicate well. Enjoy!

39

Broaden-and-build theory of positive emotions

The big idea

The broaden-and-build theory of positive emotions is concerned with help-ing us to understanding the nature and function of positive emotions. First described in 1998 by Professor Barbara Fredrickson, it suggests that emotions such as enjoyment, happiness, joy and anticipation broaden awareness, encouraging experimentation and exploration of the wider world (Fredrickson, 1998). Over time, this way of living and behaving builds skills and resilience that long outlast the initial buzz of positive emotion. Hence, the combina-tion of *broadening* of experience and *building* of capacity. For example, if a person enjoys good food they may develop an interest in how it is cooked. This in turn can lead to taking cookery classes or becoming more experi-mental with their cooking.

The theory contrasts this type of outcome with the impact of negative emotions such as fear and anger, which narrow people's attention. When experiencing these emotions, people tend to deal with specific perceived threats and problems using a limited number of coping strategies. Positive emotions open up the possibility of greater creativity while negative ones reduce creativity. However, Fredrickson's theory still finds a useful place for negative emotions. The argument is that the creative process follows two broad stages. Initially, when experiencing positive emotion a person opens up their thinking in an unfocused way to a wide range of possibilities. Negative emotions enable more detailed attention to be given to the specifics of whatever they have observed or created. Both have value depending on the task which we are trying to undertake.

So what?

There is a range of practical implications that flow from the theory. The ability to develop creativity is one. Positive emotions encourage a much broader consideration of the environment and an ability to adapt to it more readily (Fredrickson and Branigan, 2003). In a rapidly changing business context this seems to be of considerable potential value for managers and leaders.

Some research suggests that memory is enhanced through positive emotion (Talarico, Berntsen and Rubin, 2009). People experiencing positive emotions seem to notice and remember more extraneous details. Those gripped by anger or fear have their attention solely focused on what is provoking these feelings.

Feeling in a good mood at work can make you more open to receiving and accepting feedback from colleagues; this is the interesting finding from research conducted in a hospital context (Estrada, Isen and Young, 1997). Building on this, Frederickson and colleagues noticed that positive emotions tend to help build close relationships. In part this is because individuals experiencing positive emotions have the capacity to see the bigger picture, including how others relate to them. There is a greater openness to the possibility of relationship (Waugh and Fredrickson, 2006). The emotional mood managers help create in the workplace can either support or hinder the development of supportive relationships. This common sense is now supported by evidence!

In the past few years, research effort has focused on establishing whether or not there is a connection between positive emotions and people's resilience in the face of adversity. Studies have confirmed that positive emotions can help build a range of coping mechanisms (Cohn *et al*, 2009; Tugade and Frederickson, 2007).

How happiness actually happens is covered in a wide range of literature. Researchers working in the field of positive psychology like Fredrickson have identified meditation, reflective writing and religious practice as some of the means by which positive emotions can be enhanced (Fredrickson, 2002).

What else?

Recent research suggests that Frederickson's assumption that positive emotion increases a person's span of attention is not completely correct. It appears that the intensity of feeling, either positive or negative, is the key. The greater the intensity of emotions the more likely that a person will focus on specific details. A moderate intensity of feeling, either negative or positive, will enable people to perceive the bigger picture (Gable and Harmon-Jones, 2010).

Recent developments in understanding how the brain works confirm that there are some neurological factors to take into account. Unfocused exploration of ideas and feeling seems to take place largely in the right side of the brain while detailed processing happens in the left (Hoppe and Kyle, 1990; Rathunde, 2000).

These ideas have not been without their critics. Fineman, for example, highlights what he sees as the sidelining of negative feelings as being flawed. He argues that so-called negative emotions can hold the key to improved organizational performance rather than the opposite. He challenges psychologists like Fredrickson, who take the positive perspective, about their negative attitudes towards those who express negative feelings. He describes this as an 'unarticulated dark side to positiveness' and suggests that positive psychology often reflects US cultural norms rather than a more universal approach (Fineman, 2006).

Leadership challenge

Think of three good things which have happened today, and make a note of each at the end of the day. Repeat this for each day of the coming week. At the end of the week, how has this focus influenced the way you view life's events?

More help

Key references

Fredrickson, B L (1998) What good are positive emotions? *Review of General Psychology*, 2 (3), pp 300–19

Fredrickson, B L and Branigan, C (2003) Positive emotions broaden the scope of attention and thought–action repertoires, *Cognition and Emotion*, 19 (3), pp 313–32

Cohn, M A, Fredrickson, B L, Brown, S L *et al* (2009) Happiness unpacked: positive emotions increase life satisfaction by building resilience, *Emotion*, 9 (3), pp 361–8

Other references

Estrada, C A, Isen, A M and Young, M J (1997) Positive affect facilitates integration of information and decreases anchoring in reasoning among physicians, *Organizational Behavior and Human Decision Processes*, 72 (1), pp 117–35

Fineman, S (2006) On being positive: concerns and counterpoints, *The Academy of Management Review*, 31 (2), pp 270–91

Fredrickson, B L (2002) How does religion benefit health and well-being? Are positive emotions active ingredients? *Psychological Inquiry*, 13 (3), pp 209–13

Gable, P and Harmon-Jones, E (2010) The blues broaden, but the nasty narrows, *Psychological Science*, 21 (2), pp 211–15

Gable, P A and Harmon-Jones, E (2010) The effect of low versus high approach-motivated positive affect on memory for peripherally versus centrally presented information, *Emotion*, **10** (4), pp 599–603

Hoppe, K D and Kyle, N L (1990) Dual brain, creativity, and health, *Creativity Research Journal*, **3** (2), pp 150–7

Rathunde, K (2000) Broadening and narrowing in the creative process: a commentary on Fredrickson's' broaden-and-build' model, *Prevention and Treatment*, **3** (1)

Talarico, J M, Berntsen, D and Rubin, D C (2009) Positive emotions enhance recall of peripheral details, *Cognition and Emotion*, **23** (2), pp 380–98

Tugade, M M and Fredrickson, B L (2007) Regulation of positive emotions: emotion regulation strategies that promote resilience, *Journal of Happiness Studies*, **8** (3), pp 311–33

Waugh, C E and Fredrickson, B L (2006) Nice to know you: positive emotions, self–other overlap, and complex understanding in the formation of a new relationship, *Journal of Positive Psychology*, **1** (2), pp 93–106

40

What can organizations do to transform the way they think and act?

Appreciative inquiry

The big idea

A relatively straightforward definition of appreciative inquiry (AI) is 'the study and exploration of what gives life to human systems when they function at their best' (Whitney, Trosten-Bloom and Cooperrider, 2010: 1). However, a number of texts elaborate on this to try to capture something of the philosophy and practices encapsulated by the term. For example, Cooperrider *et al* say that AI is 'the co-operative co-evolutionary search for the best in people, their organizations, and the world around them... it involves the art and practice of asking questions that strengthen a system's capacity to apprehend, anticipate and heighten positive potential' (Cooperrider *et al*, 2008: 16).

AI is based on five core principles:

1 The Constructionist Principle. Reality as we know it is a subjective state rather than an objective one.

2 The Principle of Simultaneity. Inquiry is intervention and creates change. They happen at the same time, not in stages. The moment we begin to ask a question we begin to create change.

3 The Poetic Principle. Human organizations are an open book and their stories are constantly being co-authored. Pasts, presents and futures are endless sources of learning, inspiration or interpretation.

We have a choice about what we study, and what we study changes organizations.

4 The Anticipatory Principle. Human systems move in the direction of their images of the future. The more positive and hopeful the image of the future the more positive the present-day action.

5 The Positive Principle. Momentum for large-scale change requires large amounts of positive affect and social bonding. This momentum is best generated through positive questions that amplify the positive core of an organization.

(Adapted from Cooperrider *et al*, 2008 and Whitney *et al*, 2010)

The suggestion is that the combination of appreciation (an attitude of mind and heart) with inquiry (a set of practices and processes) produces a vital and powerful catalytic effect on leadership and organizational change. AI taps into people's stories about their organization at its best and unleashes information and commitment that together generate energy for positive change. Supporting human behavioural change through this strengths-based approach has similarities with some of the principles and practices adopted by positive psychology.

So what?

The application of AI within an organizational or system context is often a five-phase process. The first involves a shared agreement among leaders and staff about the overarching theme, or topic. The defining of a question is a skill in itself and careful consideration needs to be given to framing the question.

The subsequent stages are often described as the 4Ds of AI (Figure 40.1):

1 Discovery. This phase focuses on helping people tell their stories about when they experienced the topic of the inquiry at its best. This may range from an aspect of customer service through to the work of the whole organization. Appreciative interviews, where people within the organization interview one another to elicit stories of great performance, are often used for this purpose.

2 Dream. The 'data' collected in the first stage are then used to help people, in conversation with one another, to 'build on what people have discovered about the organization at its best and projecting this into their wishes, hopes and aspirations for the organization's future' (Lewis *et al* 2008: 55). Such dreams are not abstract but rather grounded in people's past experiences.

3 Design. This stage is concerned with shared decision making about how to make the dream a reality in their context. 'The Design phase defines the basic structure that will allow the dream to become

FIGURE 40.1 Five stages of AI

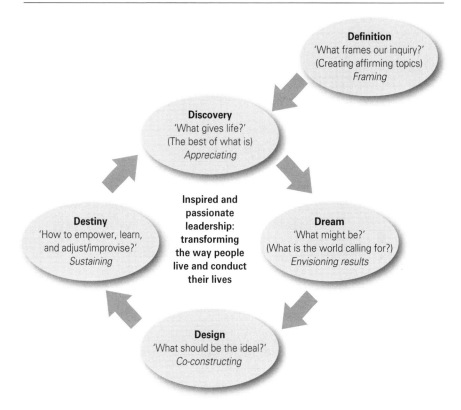

a reality. Like the other phases, the Design phase requires widespread dialogue about the nature of the structure and processes. This is what is meant by co-constructing the organization's future' (Cooperrider *et al*, 2008).

4 Destiny. Finally groups or individuals are encouraged to take forward the actions identified during the previous phases and make them a tangible reality alongside the shifts of mindset and attitude that will have taken place in the conversations during the process. A closing celebration is often held (Lewis, Passmore and Cantore, 2008).

The process is not intended to be rigid but to be flexible and iterative.

What else?

AI is not without its critics. Some suggest that by its very nature the evidence for change is highly subjective and without a proper research base. Some research has been done to review change processes supported by AI and assess their impact (Bushe and Kassam, 2005). The findings suggest that AI has been used very effectively for both transformational and non-transformational purposes. A further challenge is that given AI's origins in the United States, the concepts, values and language sound inappropriate in some contexts (Fineman, 2006). Overall, though, the experience of using AI in a wide range of contexts suggests that it is a powerful process for shifting mindsets and changing behaviours across organizations.

Leadership challenge

Use AI to lead a change exercise on a current organizational project which you are responsible for. At the end of the project, reflect on the impact AI methods had on the project and employee engagement.

More help

Key reference

Lewis, S, Passmore, J and Cantore, S (2008) *Appreciative Inquiry for Change Management: Using AI to facilitate organizational development*, Kogan Page, London

Other references

Bushe, G R and Kassam, A F (2005) When is appreciative inquiry transformational? A meta-case analysis, *Journal of Applied Behavioral Science*, **41** (2), pp 161–81
Cooperrider, D L, Whitney, D, Stavros, J M *et al* (2008) *Appreciative Inquiry Handbook: For leaders of change*, Berrett-Koehler, San Francisco
Fineman, S (2006) On being positive: concerns and counterpoints, *Academy of Management Review*, **31** (2), pp 270–91
Watkins, J and Mohr, B (2001) *Appreciative Inquiry: Change at the speed of imagination*, Berrett-Koehler, San Francisco
Whitney, D, Trosten-Bloom, A and Cooperrider, D (2010) *The Power of Appreciative Inquiry: A practical guide to positive change*, Berrett-Koehler, San Francisco

How do people's expectations of their employers affect the way they work?

41

Psychological contract

The big idea

The term 'psychological contract' broadly describes 'an individual's subjective belief in the reciprocal nature of the exchange relationship between himself/ herself and a third party (usually an employer), based on the promises made or implied in their interactions' (Rousseau, 2003). There is a wide range of definitions and perspectives, which suggests that 'psychological contract' has become an umbrella term for a range of ideas.

The main idea has been around since the early 1960s when a number of organizational and work psychology theorists, including Edgar Schein, Chris Argyris and Harold Levinson, drew attention to the relationship between workers' expectations, leadership styles and positive mental health in the workplace (Roehling, 1997). Interest in the concept has grown since the economic turmoil of the early 1990s and there now exists a sizeable body of supporting research and literature.

It was the seminal work of Professor Denise Rousseau that sparked renewed interest in the concept. She focuses on the notion that there exists between employers and employees an often unwritten set of promises about what the employer will offer the employee alongside the formal contract of employment. Such perceived promises can include opportunities for promotion, training, social contact, recognition, life–work balance and fairness in the workplace. The list is long and reflects the very wide range of expectations that people bring to their involvement with an organization. The psychological contract is said to be intensely subjective and integral to employees' expectations about what working life with an employer will be like for them.

So what?

Rousseau and others (Rousseau, 1995; Herriot and Pemberton, 1995) have identified three different types of psychological contract:

1 Relational contracts. These are based on mutual trust and a desire for stability in the relationship (social exchange). Arguably, in today's uncertain economic times, these are harder to maintain.

2 Transactional contracts. Focused on short-term specific performance measures for both parties with a recognition that, with little security of employment, there may be opportunities for monetary reward for hard work (economic exchange). These can be common when an employer is moving away from a relational type of contract.

3 Balanced contracts. Agreements which include a mutual understanding that, because of changing circumstances, the nature of the contract may also need to change: a reduction in hours worked, for example.

A fourth 'state' rather than a contract is that of 'transition' (Rousseau, 2000). This highlights the consequences of organizational change that are at odds with previously established employment arrangements.

Much of the research has focused on the impact of a breach of a promise. Robinson and Rousseau (1994) found in a study of 128 managers a perception that employers had breached the psychological contract for 70 of the managers within the first two years of employment. Breaches are much more common, it appears, than violations of the contact. Violation is the term used to describe an emotionally negative response to a breach rather than simply a shrug of the shoulders by the employee when an element of the promise is not delivered. Herriot and Pemberton (1995) describe a range of behavioural reactions to a violation which include leaving, staying and keeping your head down, and staying while taking revenge.

Zhao *et al* (2007) undertook a meta-analysis of the research about psychological contracts which indicated that the impact of strong emotional reactions on organizational outcomes is most obvious when employers are perceived to be planning a change in the rate of staff turnover (a redundancy programme, for example) and take actions that affect job satisfaction. To mitigate the danger of strong emotional reactions to breaches it is suggested that open employee communication about the nature of the psychological contract is very helpful. If employers give clear, credible explanations about what is happening, fewer employees will perceive that significant promises have been violated.

What else?

There are some criticisms of the concept. These include the view that it can be overused and that some important variables are overlooked (Arnold, 1996). It is worth noting that since an organization is not an individual it's technically unable to enter a psychological contract. There is some merit in reflecting on what organizations as entities have come to mean to people such that they are often assumed to act and relate like a real person. Generally, people think it is a very useful concept that enables managers and researchers to explore what people experience in their relationship with work and, in particular, with their employers.

Leadership challenge

What aspects of employment do you consider to be part of your formal and part of your psychological contract with your current employer? What do you think are the vital components of the psychological contract employees have with your organization? How might you influence these in the future?

More help

Key references

Roehling, M V (1997) The origins and early development of the psychological contract construct, *Journal of Management History (Archive)*, **3** (2), pp 204–17

Rousseau, D M (1989) Psychological and implied contracts in organizations, *Employee Responsibilities and Rights Journal*, **2** (2), pp 121–39

The Role of the Psychological Contract in the Contemporary Workplace. An interview with Prof Denise M Rousseau, June 2003 [accessed 20 August 2011] [Online] http://www.unfortu.net/~rafe/links/rousseau.htm

Other references

Arnold, J (1996) The psychological contract: a concept in need of closer scrutiny? *European Journal of Work and Organizational Psychology*, 5 (4), pp 511–20

Herriot, P and Pemberton, C (1995) *New Deals: The revolution in managerial careers*, John Wiley, Chichester

Robinson, S L and Rousseau, D M (1994) Violating the psychological contract: not the exception but the norm, *Journal of Organizational Behavior*, **15** (3), pp 245–59

Rousseau, D M (1995) *Psychological Contracts in Organizations: Understanding written and unwritten agreements*, Sage, Los Angeles

Rousseau, D M (2000) *Psychological Contract Inventory Technical Report*, Carnegie Mellon University, Pittsburgh, PA

Zhao, H A O, Wayne, S J, Glibkowski, B C *et al* (2007) The impact of psychological contract breach on work-related outcomes: a meta-analysis, *Personnel Psychology*, **60** (3), pp 647–80

What can you do to make training a good investment?

42

Social learning theory

The big idea

Social learning theory (SLT) suggests that human behaviour is determined by a three-way relationship between cognitive factors, environmental factors and behavioural factors. Previously, learning theories focused on two main ideas. First, the behaviourist approach, which argues that a person's behaviour is governed by past experiences that have become reinforced over time. People become conditioned and learning is only 'real' when it becomes visible in behaviours. Second, the cognitive approach, which argues that knowing how the memory works is vital in understanding how learning happens within a person's mind. Social learning theory, advocated by Albert Bandura in 1977, links these two ideas together and adds the two-way influence of the environment as a third factor. Bandura (1977) defines SLT thus: 'Social learning theory approaches the explanation of human behavior in terms of a continuous reciprocal interaction between cognitive, behavioral, and environmental determinants.'

Mind-based, or cognitive, determinants are those things we call knowledge, expectations and attitudes. Behavioural determinants are skills, practices and what Bandura calls self-efficacy, or the extent to which a person believes they can demonstrate a required behaviour in any situation. Environmental determinants are social norms, community role models, a person's ability to change the environment around them and the influence or reinforcement of others. This ability to mutually influence and shape the environment Bandura calls the principle of reciprocal determinism (Bandura, 1986). This is summarized in Figure 42.1 which shows the three-way relationship of SLT.

FIGURE 42.1   The three-way relationship of social learning theory

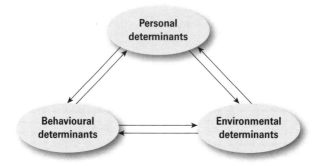

So what?

Educational and training strategies are developed and implemented based on the assumptions that people make about how learning happens. SLT is influential in the arena of training by replacing approaches that focus either on classroom-based teaching (cognitive) or developing skills by trial and error (behavioural). Bandura, and other social learning theorists, have developed some ideas that support the application of SLT to learning at work, including:

1 Workers use each other as role models and attitudes are copied and modelled between co-workers. This is particularly the case with attitudes towards the organization and aspects of the job. This means that job satisfaction is not something that comes from the intrinsic value a person feels about work but is closely connected to the attitudes of peers.

2 Goals offer a cognitive representation, or image, of the outcomes a person desires. If there is a gap between the goal and the current situation, they feel emotions and 'self-reactions' which may include changes to self-efficacy expectations. In other words, a person may find their sense of self-belief affected by what they are expected to achieve. This will impact on their determination to succeed in reaching the goal (Bandura, 2001).

3 Supervisors' behaviour is influential in modelling work values, particularly when they demonstrate consideration for their staff. This influence impacts more on staff whose self-belief is low (Weiss, 1978).

4 Human beings are able to symbolize what is happening in their environment, including at work, to help them to make sense of the present and guide them into the future.

5 Vicarious learning occurs as people learn from observing the behaviour of others.

6 Behaviour modelling happens when a trainee observes someone else receiving a reward for undertaking a task in a particular way. This behaviour is then retained and practised. Social reinforcement happens when the trainer, and other trainees, reward the trainee for imitating the desired behaviour. Finally, transfer of training takes place when the trainee incorporates the new behaviour into their usual work routine (McKenna, 2006).

A training programme based on SLT principles and focusing on, for example, team communications will include some or all of these elements:

- Trainer emphasizes desirable team communication behaviours in a brief presentation.
- Trainees watch a video of the behaviours being demonstrated in a high-performing team.
- Group discussion with the trainer about the video and the lessons that can be learned.
- Team communication role-play between trainees with feedback from trainer and the rest of the group.
- Trainees go and practise the behaviours in their workplace.
- The group meets two weeks later to discuss their experiences and how they handled them. They then each receive a certificate to recognize their achievements on the course.

(Adapted from Arnold and Randall, 2010)

What else?

There are a number of criticisms of SLT (sometimes called social cognitive theory) in the workplace. They include the view that many tasks can be done in different ways and one role model is not necessarily going to reflect this diversity (Baldwin, 1992). There are also behaviours and skills that are not amenable to role modelling, such as creativity and innovation. It's very difficult to know when someone is coming up with a good idea and role modelling will not necessarily help a company to get more of them (Gist, 1989). However, role-modelling behaviours where managers welcome new ideas when they are offered by staff are definitely very helpful in today's demanding business environment.

Leadership challenge

Review a training programme you have recently commissioned (sent members of your team on). Can you identify elements of SLT in it? What impact did these have on their learning? How can you use the insights from SLT to enhance the next training session you commission?

More help

Key references

Bandura, A (1977) *Social Learning Theory*, Prentice-Hall, Englewood Cliffs, NJ

Pajares, F (2002 [accessed 5 September 2011]) Overview of Social Cognitive Theory and of Self-Efficacy [Online] http://www.emory.edu/EDUCATION/mfp/eff.html

Other references

Arnold, J and Randall, R (2010) *Work Psychology: Understanding human behaviour in the workplace*, 5th edn, Pearson Education., Harlow

Baldwin, T T (1992) Effects of alternative modelling strategies on outcomes of interpersonal-skills training, *Journal of Applied Psychology*, 77 (2), pp 147–54

Bandura, A (1986) *Social Foundations of Thought and Action: A social cognitive theory*, Prentice-Hall, Englewood Cliffs, NJ

Bandura, A (2001) Social cognitive theory: an agentic perspective, *Annual Review of Psychology*, 52 (1), pp 1–26

Gist, M E (1989) The influence of training method selection on self-efficacy and idea generation among managers, *Personnel Psychology*, 42 (4), pp 787–805

McKenna, E F (2006) *Business Psychology and Organizational Behaviour*, 4th edn, Psychology Press, Hove, Sussex

Weiss, H M (1978) Social learning of work values in organizations, *Journal of Applied Psychology*, 63 (6), pp 711–18

How do I take account of the forces for and against change?

Force field analysis

The big idea

Force field analysis (FFA) is a practical technique frequently used in change management. It tends to be used mostly by teams and organizations planning a major change, although FFA is very flexible and can equally well be used in coaching conversations or by individuals thinking about personal change challenges.

Its creator, Kurt Lewin, was one of the main founders of social psychology. His interest was in the human aspects of change, particularly emotions, attitudes and behaviours. Lewin's basic idea is that:

> An issue is held in balance by the interaction of two opposing sets of forces – those seeking to promote change (driving forces) and those attempting to maintain the status quo (restraining forces).
>
> (Lewin, 1951)

Lewin is primarily referring to social situations involving people. He is arguing that there are many factors, often emotional or behavioural ones, that are for and against a proposed change. These need to be taken into account when planning a change. People and organizations, Lewin suggests, are naturally in a state of 'quasi-equilibrium'. To achieve change, some destabilization needs to happen by either increasing the driving forces or reducing the restraining forces; or by doing both.

This is best demonstrated in a classic FFA diagram (Figure 43.1).

FIGURE 43.1   Forces for and against change

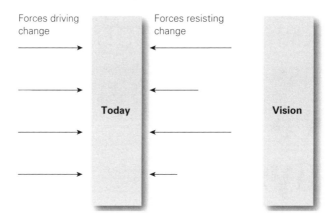

In a business context the driving forces are often identified as new technology, changing markets and innovative ideas. Restraining forces are things like individuals' fear of failure and wider organizational resistance to change. Each situation is different and FFA is there to be used by the people involved to make sense of the situation and identify what needs to be done to create positive instability most effectively. The trick is to ensure that the instability leads towards achieving a predetermined vision rather than just creating chaos.

Lewin had some interesting insights, which can get overlooked, about the way a force field works. First, increasing the driving forces will result in an increase of the resisting forces. Second, reducing resisting forces is better because it allows movement toward the vision with less tension. Third, group norms are an important force in resisting and shaping change.

FFA fits into Lewin's more comprehensive theory of change (Lewin, 1951). This he described as the unfreeze–change–freeze (refreeze) model. Using FFA, an organization or individual can plan for creative instability to shift it into a space where change can happen. Once the instability is experienced by people, change happens, followed by a period of 'freezing' where people feel things have returned to 'normal'. The trick is to ensure that people do not simply revert to doing things the old way while at the same time feeling some sense of social stability.

Since Lewin published his work in the 1940s and 1950s, many change gurus have adopted his ideas about organizational change into their own models.

So what?

The following steps are a good practical way of using FFA:

1 Define the change you want to make happen. Write this vision down and keep it at the forefront of your thinking through the exercise. You may simply wish to use FFA to diagnose the current status quo, in which case a vision will not be necessary.

2 Brainstorm the driving forces – those that are encouraging change. Put these on the left-hand side of the diagram as arrows pointing towards the centre.

3 Brainstorm the restraining forces – those that are opposing change. Put these on the right-hand side of the diagram as arrows pointing towards the centre.

4 Evaluate the strength of the driving and restraining forces. Do this by rating each force, from 1 (weak) to 5 (strong), and total each side. Or you can leave the numbers out and draw the arrows in different thicknesses to represent relative strength.

5 Review the forces. Ask which of the forces have some flexibility for change or can be influenced.

6 Strategize! Create a strategy to strengthen the driving forces or weaken the restraining forces, or both.

7 Prioritize action steps. What action steps can you take that will achieve the greatest impact? Identify the resources you will need and decide how to implement the action steps.

(Adapted from **http://www.change-management-coach.com/**)

What else?

FFA has been criticized for being simplistic, although, to be fair to Lewin, he saw it as one way of understanding, and making visible, the complex forces at work within a social 'field', not purely as a management tool. Similarly, in an environment of rapid continuous change, the unfreeze–change–freeze model is seen as too linear and assumes that a return to some sort of stable state will be possible. Usually the next change is just around the corner! Recently the idea of 'resistance to change' has been challenged (Dent and Goldberg, 1999), mainly because the phrase suggests a psychological state, which is something Lewin did not intend to convey. In more recent positive approaches to change, such as appreciative inquiry, resistance has been viewed as an energy affecting everyone and is probably closer to the idea Lewin had in mind.

To balance the criticism there are quite a few documented examples of how FFA has been used practically to good effect (Baulcomb, 2003; Kumar, 1999; Schein, 1996; Thomas, 1985).

Leadership challenge

Apply FFA to a current organizational change issue which you are leading. At the end of the process, what difference did it make to the way you handled the different stakeholders in the change process?

More help

http://www.change-management-coach.com/

Key reference

Lewin, K (1951) *Field Theory in Social Science: Selected theoretical papers*, ed D Cartwright, Harper & Row, New York

Other references

Baulcomb, J S (2003) Management of change through force field analysis, *Journal of Nursing Management*, **11** (4), pp 275–80

Dent, E B and Goldberg, S G (1999) Challenging 'resistance to change', *Journal of Applied Behavioral Science*, **35** (1), pp 25–41

Kumar, S (1999) Force field analysis: applications in PRA, *PLA Notes*, **36**, pp 17–23

Schein, E H (1996) Kurt Lewin's change theory in the field and in the classroom: notes toward a model of managed learning, *Systemic Practice and Action Research*, **9** (1), pp 27–47

Thomas, J (1985) Force field analysis: a new way to evaluate your strategy, *Long Range Planning*, **18** (6), pp 54–9

How can you make a workplace fair?

44

Organizational justice

The big idea

Organizational justice is a set of ideas about how people react to perceived fairness or unfairness in the workplace. Philosophically it has its roots in the contemplations of Socrates and other Greek thinkers who were concerned with questions about the nature of true justice (Colquitt *et al*, 2001). In practice, organizational justice focuses on what employees perceive and feel to be just or unjust and how their reactions either way can be well managed. Cropanzano, Bowen and Gilliland define it as 'a personal evaluation about the ethical and moral standing of managerial conduct' (2007: 35). Another helpful definition is that organizational justice refers to 'the extent to which employees perceive workplace procedures, interactions and outcomes to be fair in nature' (Baldwin, 2006: 2).

Business psychologists have identified three main types of organizational justice:

1 Distributive justice. This is based on the equity principle (Adams, 1965), which suggests that people judge their relationships on how fairly they think they have been rewarded for work effort when compared to the rewards received by others. Nowadays, for example, companies put in a great deal of effort to make sure job grades and salary bands are seen to be fair. Problems can still arise when, for example, one person is promoted and another isn't, even though the perception is that both have put in an equal amount of effort.

2 Procedural justice. Procedural justice is the perceived fairness of decision-making processes. People are happy to accept a decision much more readily if they believe that it was a fair process. So, an employee disappointed at not being promoted may still feel ok

about it because they see that the decision-making process was unbiased. It helps if procedures for decision making are consistent, neutral, accurate, ethical and have an appeal mechanism. People's perception of fairness will also improve if they are given a chance to present their case and participate in the process (Sisson and Storey, 2000).

3 Interactional justice. This is about the quality of the interpersonal behaviours people experience, particularly by managers, during a decision-making process (interpersonal justice). Typical of the behaviours that enhance people's perception of being treated fairly are respect, propriety, truthfulness and justification (Bies and Moag, 1986). It is also about the company sharing relevant information with employees to keep them up to date about how well the company is doing (informational justice).

So what?

The positive impact for a company of fair decision-making systems and consistent, respectful managerial behaviours is likely to be high morale and strong staff commitment. It's also likely that it will become an employer of choice, so recruiting talented staff will be less of an issue than perhaps for other companies. The implications of failing to pay attention to organizational justice range from staff reducing their work effort all the way to strikes and legal action. The literature suggests that companies should give particular attention to:

● performance appraisal – ensuring that appraisals are done on time, using well-accepted performance criteria and conducted in a polite constructive manner;

● disciplinary procedures – undertaken by managers who have had good training in the procedural and interactional justice elements of processes;

● conflict resolution – with procedures that allow for mediation and the voice of all parties to be clearly heard;

● redundancy policy – that ensures demonstrable fairness both to employees and in any court of law;

● recruitment and promotion – using job analysis and assessment techniques that enable employees to understand the basis for any decision affecting them;

● organizational change – that incorporates two-way communication and the engagement of employees in decision making.

These are all sound managerial practices. The benefits are that the company builds employee trust, improves job performance and, crucially, customer loyalty and satisfaction (Bowen, Gilliland, and Folger, 1999; Campbell and Finch, 2004; Cropanzano *et al*, 2007).

What else?

There is evidence that organizational justice, or the absence of it, has a bearing on the physical health of employees. Several studies confirm a link between perceived injustice and health (Kivimäki *et al*, 2003). Men tend to be more impacted than women and this is clearly demonstrated in a large study involving over 4,000 Whitehall civil servants (Elovainio *et al*, 2010; Kivimäki *et al*, 2004).

The concept of organizational justice is a complex one and it's not easy to map the interrelationships between each of the elements (Colquitt *et al*, 2001). Organizational justice is focused on the internal management of employees while corporate social responsibility takes similar ideas and applies them to companies' relationships with their external environment.

Leadership challenge

What actions do you need to take to apply the principles of organizational justice to your organization?

More help

Key references

Baldwin, S (2006) *Organizational Justice*, Institute for Employment Studies, Brighton, Sussex

Sisson, K and Storey, J (2000) *The Realities of Human Resource Management: Managing the employment relationship*, Open University Press, Milton Keynes

Other references

Adams, J S (1965) Inequity in social exchange in L Berkowitz, *Advances in Experimental Social Psychology*, **2**, pp 267–99

Bies, R J and Moag, J S (1986) Interactional justice: communication criteria of fairness, *Research on Negotiation in Organizations*, **1** (1), pp 43–55

Bowen, D E, Gilliland, S W and Folger, R (1999) HRM and service fairness: how being fair with employees spills over to customers, *Organizational Dynamics*, **27** (3), pp 7–23

Campbell, L and Finch, E (2004) Customer satisfaction and organizational justice, *Facilities*, **22** (7/8), pp 178–89

Colquitt, J A, Conlon, D E, Wesson, M J *et al* (2001) Justice at the millennium: a meta-analytic review of 25 years of organizational justice research, *Journal of Applied Psychology*, **86** (3), pp 425–45

Cropanzano, R, Bowen, D E and Gilliland, S W (2007) The management of organizational justice, *Academy of Management Perspectives*, **21** (4), pp 34–48

Elovainio, M, Ferrie, J E, Singh-Manoux, A *et al* (2010) Organizational justice and markers of inflammation: the Whitehall II study, *Occupational and Environmental Medicine*, **67** (2), pp 78–83

Kivimäki, M, Elovainio, M, Vahtera, J *et al* (2003) Organizational justice and health of employees: prospective cohort study, *Occupational and Environmental Medicine*, **60** (1), pp 27–34

Kivimäki, M, Ferrie, J E, Head, J *et al* (2004) Organizational justice and change in justice as predictors of employee health: the Whitehall II study, *Journal of Epidemiology and Community Health*, **58** (11), pp 931–7

How do you tackle difficult people at work?

45

Managing difficult people

The big idea

There are plenty of books on the market about how to handle difficult people at work. Surprisingly, there has been little research about what makes a person difficult or what strategies are effective in dealing with them. One of the most popular writers on this topic is Robert Bramson. His ground-breaking book *Coping with Difficult People* describes a set of seven 'difficult' personality types and their associated communication styles (Bramson, 1981). These were developed by Bramson drawing on material from 25 years of observing and talking to managers in over 200 organizations. More recently, a number of authors like Brinkman *et al* have built on his typology, although the main difference between them tends to be the labels they use for the different types (Brinkman and Kirschner, 2002).

Bramson's original typology of difficult people and their communication styles is shown in Table 45.1.

So what?

For each type of difficult person a range of handling strategies is offered (Table 45.2).

TABLE 45.1   Bramson's original typology of difficult people and their communication styles

Type	Communication style
Hostile/aggressive (Tank)	Attacking or bullying. Uses controlling language and behaviours.
Complaining (Whiner)	Whining and fault finding. Uses 'yes but' statements quite frequently.
Unresponsive (Nothing person)	One-word replies such as yes or no if a response to a question is given at all. Will often just shrug their shoulders.
Super-agreeable (Yes person)	Always tells the listener what they think they want to hear.
Negative (No person)	Uses the language of failure. Every project not their own is likely to fail.
Know-it-all (Think they know it all)	Ready with a definitive answer for every question.
Indecisive (Maybe person)	Unable to come to a conclusion or decision.

SOURCE: adapted from Raynes (2001). Terms in brackets are those used by Brinkman and Kirschner (2002) in their alternative typology.

TABLE 45.2   The handling strategies for each type of person

Type	Handling strategy
Hostile/aggressive (Tank)	Stand up to them but let them vent (some suggest interrupt them). Provide clear feedback on the impact of their behaviour.
Complaining (Whiner)	Listen but don't agree with them. Shift quickly to problem solving.
Unresponsive (Nothing person)	Use open-ended questions to draw them out. A friendly silent stare may also help.
Super-agreeable (Yes person)	Assume that behaviour is an attempt to win approval. Give honest feedback and assure them that you respect their honesty.
Negative (No person)	Try not to get drawn in, and restate your own optimism.
Know-it-all (Think they know it all)	Don't challenge their views directly but do set out the facts. Create ways in which they can save face.
Indecisive (Maybe person)	Set out the issues and make it safe for them to make mistakes.

SOURCE: adapted from Raynes (2001). Terms in brackets are those used by Brinkman and Kirschner (2002) in their alternative typology.

The general assumption is that, in spite of their difficult behaviours, these employees are valuable to the company and need to be retained. This leads organizations to encourage fellow 'good' employees to accommodate them by adjusting their own behaviour. It's assumed that as they do this, the behaviours of their difficult colleagues will ultimately change. As a consequence, the employer does not need to attempt to help change the behaviour of the difficult person.

One option is for employers to screen people for potential difficult behaviours in advance of employment. Given that research tells us that previous employer references are of limited use, psychological tests may offer an option. Two types of test are identified by Raynes (2001) as offering potentially suitable measures. The first type, like the Radford Inventory, seeks to identify levels of self-esteem. The theory behind this is that most difficult behaviour appears directly related to people's self-esteem. The lower the sense of self-esteem the more likely that difficult behaviours will manifest themselves. There is, however, some evidence that high self-esteem is linked to bullying and aggressive communication styles. The second type of test is a vocational interest survey such as the Aamodt Vocational Interest Survey (AVIS). This gives employers an understanding of what type of work motivates people. High levels of motivation and interest in a job have been implicitly linked with the expression of appropriate helpful communication styles to match the context.

Understanding how managers and supervisors respond to difficult behaviours is a key issue. O'Reilly III and Weitz (1980) identified a high degree of variability between managers in response to what they call 'marginal' employees. Some managers find applying sanctions to employees a personally painful process, while others have no difficulty in disciplining or sacking someone. One thing that managers tend to underestimate is the symbolic value of disciplinary action for the performance of a group. So, according to the research, issuing a warning to someone for 'difficult' behaviour is likely to result in enhanced group performance. They make the point that 'difficult' behaviour by a single employee should not be considered in isolation from their social context.

Lubit (2004) suggests that one of the key routes to handling difficult behaviours by so-called toxic managers or employees is to understand what lies behind them, design appropriate interventions and take control of your own feelings and behaviours so that what you do is most effective.

What else?

A criticism of Bramson's original model is that it tends to stereotype people. In reality, individuals can express a number of 'difficult' behaviours depending on mood and context. The ideas, while intuitively attractive, are not based on formal research findings. In particular, there is no solid evidence that the suggested handling strategies actually work. Taking action against one individual can have unforeseen consequences, both for that person and for the wider work group. Sometimes this is positive, but it can also be negative and affect existing psychological frailty. The linkages between work, the individual's self-esteem and their behaviour are also not particularly clear (Raynes, 2001).

There is a range of other factors that impact on behaviour, including stress and medical conditions such as depression that need to be taken into account when handling a person displaying difficult behaviours.

Leadership challenge

As a leader, when have you had to deal with difficult people? What approaches were more successful and why? What lessons do you draw about how to manage 'difficult' people in the future?

More help

Key reference

Bramson, R (1981) *Coping with Difficult People*, Dell, New York

Other references

Brinkman, R and Kirschner, R (2002) *Dealing with People You Can't Stand: How to bring out the best in people at their worst*, McGraw-Hill Professional, New York

Lubit, R (2004) The tyranny of toxic managers: applying emotional intelligence to deal with difficult personalities, *Ivey Business Journal*, **68** (4), pp 1–7

O'Reilly III, C A and Weitz, B A (1980) Managing marginal employees: the use of warnings and dismissals, *Administrative Science Quarterly*, **25**, pp 467–84

Raynes, B L (2001) Predicting difficult employees: the relationship between vocational interests, self-esteem, and problem communication styles, *Applied HRM Research*, **6** (1), pp 33–66

46

The bounded rationality model of decision making

The big idea

'How do people really make decisions?' was the question Herbert Simon, a noted professor of economics, considered when he came up with the idea of bounded rationality. He proposed that instead of always following a rational linear process, decision making is often constrained by time pressures, people's thought processes and the limited amount of available information (Simon, 1957). People, he concluded, managers in organizations included, lacked the resources and ability to reach the best solution and instead applied their decision-making processes to choices that they had already greatly simplified. This he called satisficing, or being happy with a satisfactory decision rather than the absolute best one. Simon's model incorporates the idea that people employ cognitive 'shortcuts' or heuristics when making decisions. Heuristics are well-developed thought processes that 'guide the search for alternatives into areas where there is a good chance of finding a satisfactory solution' (McKenna, 2006).

Bounded rationality, as a model of decision making applied to the business world, has three principal components:

1 The consideration of alternative solutions in sequence. In an ideal and relatively stable world managers will survey the business environment, identify threats and use extensive information sources to consider all possible responses. This reflects the econological model of decision making, which emphasizes a linear and rational approach (Behling and Schriesheim, 1976). In this model it is

assumed that all options will be considered before evaluation. Bounded rationality, on the other hand, suggests that managers in unstable environments have a tendency to discard alternatives as they go through a list of options. They may use criteria against which they assess the options but they do not always consider the merits of all options relative to each other.

2 The use of heuristics. These cognitive 'shortcuts' reduce the number of alternatives managers need to work through to come up with a solution (Simon and Newell, 1971). They don't aim to come up with the best solution, but a satisfactory one given the circumstances.

Tversky *et al* offer three types of heuristics:

2.1 Representative heuristic. Managers use this type of heuristic when they estimate the probability of an event happening. So, for example, a supplier who has had a history of reliability may, if they are awarded a new contract for a larger volume of goods, be assumed to be reliable on the basis of probability.

2.2 Availability heuristic. Managers use experiences from their memory to make assumptions about what will happen in the future. This can lead to bias and potential error. So, for example, a manager who takes responsibility for a new staff team may assume that the positive dynamics she experienced with an apparently similar team will be replicated in the new team.

2.3 Anchoring-and-adjustment heuristic. Managers can have a tendency to latch onto a piece of existing information which they then use to bias their final decision regardless of any more recent information. This can lead to an innate conservatism in, for example, investment decisions. Managers assume, for example, that the rate of growth in a sector means that £x of investment in machinery is reasonable when, in fact, new information suggests that the market is growing much more strongly and £y investment is more appropriate to take full advantage of these new conditions.

(Tversky and Kahneman, 1974)

3 Satisficing. At its core, satisficing is about managers accepting a satisfactory outcome rather than the best. This also implies that they spend less time and money on gathering information than they otherwise might. Simon's model suggests that, behaviourally, managers may start out looking for the best outcome but as they fail to find it, for whatever reasons, their aspirations are knocked back and they accept second best. This then risks becoming a pattern of managerial decision-making behaviour (Simon, 1957).

So what?

Complexity and uncertainty are evidently an integral aspect of the bounded rationality model. This has led to recognizing that managerial intuition has a role to play in decision making. Robbins (2003) suggests that intuition in a managerial context is an unconscious process created out of distilled experiences that can complement systematic analysis. So, in what contexts might managers use intuition in decision making? Agor suggests times when:

- information is fairly limited;
- uncertainty is high and there are few precedents;
- data available are mainly qualitative rather than quantitative;
- time in which to reach a final decision is limited;
- there are many equally attractive options.

(Adapted from Agor, 1986)

It is worth noting that while the bounded rationality model is particularly interesting because of the insights it offers into managerial behaviours, there are other decision-making models that also give helpful perspectives. There are two types of decision: structured or unstructured.

The structured decision is well defined in terms of process and expected outcome. The decision cycle and the econological model are two examples of approaches that managers can take when making structured decisions. These models favour a linear approach, with rationality and logicality as their guiding principles.

An unstructured decision is one that is perceived to be unique and needs to be taken in conditions of high uncertainty. In this instance managers may adopt bounded rationality, the 'implicit favourite' model or negotiation. The implicit favourite model suggests that before any process starts a manager has already decided the alternative they intend to choose. In negotiation the decision-making process embraces a range of parties and is often concerned both with the final decision and with the implementation process (McKenna, 2006).

What else?

In reality, managers may adopt a combination of models and behaviours to inform their individual decision-making practice. Organizational, legislative, regulatory and environmental factors are also likely to impact on how managers behave when faced with different types of decision at different times.

There are some critiques of the bounded rationality model in the literature. Kaufman (1999) suggests that satisficing tends to be an emotional response by managers rather than a cognitive one as originally proposed by Simon. Behling and Schriesheim (1976) argue that the dividing line between bounded rationality and more structured decision-making models is not as definite as might appear at first sight, as there are often components of both models found in managerial behaviour.

Leadership challenge

What insights does this model give you about how you make decisions? What can you do to make better decisions?

More help

Key reference

Simon, H A (1957) *Models of Man: Social and rational; mathematical essays on rational human behavior in a social setting*, Wiley, New York

Other references

Agor, W H (1986) How top executives use their intuition to make important decisions, *Business Horizons*, **29** (1), pp 49–53

Behling, O and Schriesheim, C (1976) *Organizational Behavior: Theory, research, and application*, Allyn & Bacon, Boston

Kaufman, B E (1999) Emotional arousal as a source of bounded rationality, *Journal of Economic Behavior and Organization*, **38** (2), pp 135–44

McKenna, E F (2006) *Business Psychology and Organizational Behaviour*, 4th edn, Psychology Press, Hove, Sussex

Robbins, S P (2003) *Organisational Behaviour: Global and Southern African perspectives*, Pearson Education South Africa, Cape Town

Simon, H A and Newell, A (1971) Human problem solving: the state of the theory in 1970, *American Psychologist*, **26** (2), pp 145–59

Tversky, A and Kahneman, D (1974) Judgment under uncertainty: heuristics and biases, *Science*, **185** (4157), pp 1124–31

47

Conversational approaches to change

The big idea

Interest in the contribution that conversations make to effective organizational change has grown in recent years. For example, educator and consultant Carolyn Baldwin defines conversational leadership as: 'The leaders' intentional use of conversation as a core process to cultivate the collective intelligence needed to create business and social value' (Hurley and Brown, 2009).

The argument is that leaders who take a conversational approach to their work can address complex issues more effectively and cost-efficiently. Conversational leadership envisages that a leader of change will be competent and confident in using powerful questions and 'collaborative social technologies' to enable collective wisdom and action to become manifest. This approach is in striking contrast to many of the directive, top-down, linear change models that have pervaded Western organizational psychology during the past hundred or so years. It is underpinned by social constructionist theory, which argues that social reality is a shared co-constructed reality. The process of co-construction takes place in the daily routine conversations between people and in what social psychologist Kenneth Gergen describes as transformative dialogue (Gergen, McNamee and Barrett, 2001). Such dialogue, or conversation, creates new and shared understanding between people who previously held very different perspectives. In social constructionist thinking this change in understanding also represents a change in reality. Conversation and action are therefore inextricably intertwined.

There are a growing number of processes that help enable organizational conversation. Two, World Café and Open Space, are featured in this chapter.

World Café

By re-creating a café atmosphere, anywhere between 12 and 1,500 people can feel relaxed and encouraged to have a series of 20- to 30-minute conversations around a question that matters. Volunteer table hosts remain at the tables to connect conversations while participants move twice or three times to new tables. At the end of each round of conversations the café host facilitates a whole café conversation that surfaces underlying themes and key insights. The process can then be repeated with a new question.

There are a number of principles that underpin this approach:

- Setting the context. Begin by clarifying the purpose and broad parameters within which the conversations will take place. This theme should be set out on invitations to the café and repeated at the start of the event.

- Creating hospitable space. Using music and room decoration, people arrive into a space that is different from that which they normally experience. The intention is to create a café type of environment that encourages relaxation and a sense of being at ease.

- Explore questions that matter. Focus collective attention on powerful questions that build engagement and a sense of inquiry.

- Encourage everyone's contribution. The host invites full participation through careful listening and speaking with intention.

- Connect diverse perspectives. Through intentionally creating diversity by inviting many perspectives into the café, build the density of connections among people while retaining a common focus on core questions.

- Listen together for patterns, insights and deeper questions. Focus attention on common themes without losing individual contribution.

- Harvest and share collective discoveries. Make collective knowledge and insight visible and actionable.

(Adapted from Brown and Isaacs, 2005)

Open Space

Open Space begins with self-selected participants, meeting in a circle, invited to consider a predetermined theme, moves on to working with a community bulletin board and then a marketplace that helps participants structure their own agendas and meetings. A series of self-managed conversations, usually lasting about one and a half hours, then follows, and the event concludes with participants back in a circle, each given an opportunity to make a closing comment. An Open Space event can last half a day or as long as three days depending on the issues being considered.

As its name implies, Open Space has a very loose structure and relies on people taking their own responsibility for hosting conversations on subjects that matter to them. The interventions by the facilitator are very minimal. Their prime role is to 'hold the space', thereby allowing participants to enjoy the freedom to converse.

Open Space operates with four principles:

- Whoever come are the right people.
- Whatever happens is the only thing that could have happened.
- Whenever it starts is the right time.
- When it's over, it's over.

And the Law (!) of Two Feet: If during the course of the gathering any person finds themselves in a situation in which they are neither learning nor contributing they are invited to use their two feet and go to a more productive place.

During Open Space events, conversation hosts are encouraged to take notes which are used to write up a final report of proceedings (Owen, 2008).

So what?

World Café

A World Café is most appropriate when:

- You want to encourage the sharing of knowledge and an in-depth exploration of key challenges and opportunities.
- People need encouragement to engage in meaningful conversation with one another for the first time.
- It is important to build mutual ownership of outcomes.

A World Café is not so appropriate when:

- A solution to a challenge has already been predetermined.
- There is a very limited amount of time available.
- You want to make detailed implementation plans.
- People have already taken highly polarized positions around the questions you are proposing.

Open Space

An Open Space event is most appropriate when:

- A diverse group of people must deal with complex and potentially conflicting material in innovative and productive ways.
- People want to give time and energy to real-life issues which are of passionate concern to those involved.
- You have short timescales and want to create a very engaging and empowering environment.

An Open Space is not so appropriate when:

- A decision has already been made and people have limited opportunity to influence outcomes.
- Leaders want a strong degree of control over the agenda.
- There is lack of clarity about the theme of the event.
- A suitable physical space with many breakout areas cannot be identified.
- There is a need to present a significant volume of material to an audience in advance.

(Adapted from Lewis, Passmore and Cantore, 2008)

What else?

At present, very little formal scientific research has been undertaken on the effectiveness of conversational approaches to change. What evaluation exists tends to be in the form of extended case studies (Brown and Isaacs, 2005; Lewis *et al*, 2008). Given that appreciative inquiry is also a conversationally based approach to change, Bushe's meta-analysis is also relevant (Bushe and Kassam, 2005). The findings indicate that conversation is a powerful vehicle for change. Experience suggests that some organizations find using conversation problematic because it is culturally different, can challenge power structures and bring to the surface difficult-to-manage relational issues (Lewis *et al*, 2008).

Leadership challenge

Use one of these approaches to enable conversations to happen in your organization. What happened?

More help

http://www.theworldcafe.com
http://www.openspaceworld.org

Key reference

Lewis, S, Passmore, J and Cantore, S (2008) *Appreciative Inquiry for Change Management: Using AI to facilitate organizational development*, Kogan Page, London

Other references

Brown, J and Isaacs, D (2005) *The World Café: Shaping our futures through conversations that matter*, Berrett-Koehler, San Francisco

Bushe, G R and Kassam, A F (2005) When is appreciative inquiry transformational? A meta-case analysis, *Journal of Applied Behavioral Science*, **41** (2), pp 161–81

Gergen, K J, McNamee, S and Barrett, F J (2001) Toward transformative dialogue, *International Journal of Public Administration*, **24** (7/8), pp 679–708

Hurley, T J and Brown, J (2009) Conversational leadership: thinking together for change, *The Systems Thinker*, **20** (9), pp 2–8

Owen, H (2008) *Open Space Technology: A user's guide*, Berrett-Koehler, San Francisco

48

How can metaphors help managers change their organizations?

Organizational metaphors

The big idea

In 1986 Gareth Morgan, a professor of organizational behaviour, published a landmark book, *Images of Organization*, in which he argues that all theories of organization and management are based on implicit images or metaphors that shape the way people see, understand and manage organizations (Morgan, 1986). This popular book goes on to suggest that when managers interpret the characteristics of an organization using one particular metaphor, they inevitably ignore other metaphors that offer a different perspective. In other words, managers' views are always partial and never complete.

Morgan fleshes out his argument by saying that people, and managers in an organizational context, use metaphor as a way of understanding one experience relative to another. So when a manager says, or assumes, that an organization operates like a machine, they have in their minds an understanding of the characteristics of a machine and how it compares with their experience of organizational life. The reality, however, is that an organization has components a machine obviously doesn't have, such as human beings with emotions and independent wills! This is the partial view to which Morgan draws attention.

Needless to say, if managers really just used a machine metaphor to guide their behaviours and attitudes, the implications would be far-reaching for their staff and the wider organization. Morgan says that this is the paradox of metaphor. It gives powerful insight and at the same time can become a distortion – a way of not seeing what is really there. From this perspective he suggests that no one theory or metaphor will ever be sufficient for structuring the understanding of organization and management.

Morgan draws upon the philosophical and linguistic perspectives of George Lakoff and Mark Johnson, who argued:

> In all aspects of life... we define our reality in terms of metaphors and then proceed to act on the basis of the metaphors. We draw inferences, set goals, make commitments, and execute plans, all on the basis of how we in part structure our experience, consciously and unconsciously, by means of metaphor.
>
> (Lakoff and Johnson, 1980)

Other influential thinkers such as Cassirer and Black have also explored the way that metaphors may define how people understand their world (Black, 1962; Cassirer, 1946). Organizational theorists, argues Morgan, consistently use their own metaphors with the aim of offering the world an ultimate theory about how organizations work. This approach can be traced back to the machine metaphor that underpins the work of classical management theorists such as Frederick Taylor and Henri Fayol (Fayol, 1949; Taylor, 1911) through to the more recent organizational metaphors like the complexity imagery of Ralph Stacey (Stacey, 1996) and the conversational constructs of Patricia Shaw (Shaw, 2002).

So what?

In *Images of Organization*, Morgan offers a description of eight common metaphors and associated concepts used by theorists and managers. The list is also a typology of metaphors, albeit perhaps now a little out of date given the plethora of metaphors which continue to emerge.

Morgan's metaphors for organizations are:

- *Machines*. Efficiency, waste, maintenance, order, clockwork, cogs in a wheel, programmes, inputs and outputs, standardization, production, measurement and control, design.
- *Organisms*. Living systems, environmental conditions, adaptation, life cycles, recycling, needs, homeostasis, evolution, survival of the fittest, health, illness.
- *Brains*. Learning, parallel information processing, distributed control, mindsets, intelligence, feedback, requisite variety, knowledge, networks.
- *Cultures*. Society, values, beliefs, laws, ideology, rituals, diversity, traditions, history, service, shared vision and mission, understanding, qualities, families.
- *Political systems*. Interests and rights, power, hidden agendas and back-room deals, authority, alliances, party line, censorship, gatekeepers, leaders, conflict management.
- *Psychic prisons*. Conscious and unconscious processes, repression and regression, ego, denial, projection, coping and defence mechanisms, pain and pleasure principle, dysfunction, workaholism.

- *Flux and transformation.* Constant change, dynamic equilibrium, flow, self-organization, systemic wisdom, attractors, chaos, complexity, butterfly effect, emergent properties, dialectics, paradox.
- *Instruments of domination.* Alienation, repression, imposing values, compliance, charisma, maintenance of power, force, exploitation, divide and rule, discrimination, corporate interest.

(Adapted from Morgan, 1986)

Morgan argues that using these metaphors will stimulate metaphoric thinking and enable managers to both interpret their organizational context with new perspectives and prompt creativity in exploring and describing what the future might look like.

What else?

There is some criticism that Morgan's list of metaphors has, in itself, become a hindrance to helping managers develop their own metaphorical thinking. The argument is that managers tend to cite one of Morgan's metaphors rather than constructing their own (McCourt, 1997). Metaphors by their very nature have their limitations and overextending their use can lead to misunderstandings (Makin, Cooper and Cox, 1996). There is also a danger that organizational metaphors become the domain and language of management consultants offering superficial organizational 'diagnostics' without a deeper understanding of how changing metaphors actually may, or may not, lead to improved business results.

Leadership challenge

What are the metaphors used to describe your organization? Do these need to change to reflect the future business challenges? How might you do this?

More help

Key reference

Morgan, G (1986) *Images of Organization*, Sage, Thousand Oaks, CA

Other references

Black, M (1962) *Models and metaphors*, Cornell University Press, Ithaca, NY
Cassirer, E (1946) *Language and Myth*, trans S K Langer, Dover, New York

Fayol, H (1949) *General and Industrial Administration*, Sir Isaac Pitman and Sons, London

Lakoff, G and Johnson, M (1980) *Metaphors We Live By*, Chicago University Press, Chicago

Makin, P J, Cooper, C L and Cox, C (1996) *Organizations and the Psychological Contract: Managing people at work*, Blackwell, Oxford

McCourt, W (1997) Discussion note: using metaphors to understand and to change organizations: a critique of Gareth Morgan's approach, *Organization Studies*, **18** (3), pp 511–22

Shaw, P (2002) *Changing Conversations in Organizations: A complexity approach to change*, Psychology Press, Hove, Sussex

Stacey, R D (1996) *Complexity and Creativity in Organizations*, Berrett-Koehler, San Francisco

Taylor, F W (1911) *Scientific Management*, Harper and Brothers, New York

49

How can you make work less stressful?

The vitamin model of stress

The big idea

In 2009/10 the UK Health and Safety Executive reported that 9.8 million working days were lost that year because of work-related stress, depression or anxiety (**http://www.hse.gov.uk/**). Workplace accidents came second in the list of work-related causes for absence. In the United States, comparative and definitive figures are difficult to find but quoted figures suggest that billions of dollars are lost to industry each year through stress-related absence. If you set aside the financial cost to business, the human cost for employees is also considerable. The impact on morale and commitment to achieving company goals cannot be overestimated.

Stress in the workplace can be defined from a psychological perspective as 'intervening psychological processes that link exposure to work-related problems to the negative impact of those problems' (Arnold and Randall, 2010: 435). Stress manifests itself as a negative emotional state that results from the interaction between a person and their environment. It can result in a range of psychological, physical health and organizational health problems. Professor Peter Warr, in the development of what became known as the Warr vitamin model of stress, suggests that job characteristics have a direct link with the mental health of the job holder.

Warr's model is based on an analogy between how vitamins work in the realm of human physical health. Vitamins A and D, for example, are essential for human health but when consumed in too great a quantity they become harmful. Vitamins C and E, on the other hand, cause no ill effects even when consumed to excess. Similarly, the psychological characteristics of the environment vary in terms of impact. Warr argues that some may cause no harm even if experienced in great quantities by employees. Examples include esteem and the perceived meaningfulness of the job. Other characteristics, such as variety in the job and externally generated demands, are likely to cause no difficulty, and even add to job satisfaction, until they exceed a certain point when they become unhelpful and even damaging to psychological well-being. Having too little of a job characteristic such as task variety can also lead to stress through boredom and under-stimulation. Each of the 'vitamins' brings benefits for individuals but only in the right quantities (Warr, 1986, 1994).

The original model had nine elements and has subsequently been extended to twelve (Table 49.1). The initials beside each element indicate if it is a harm-free positive characteristic (CE) or harmful if levels become excessive or negligible (AD).

TABLE 49.1   The Warr vitamin model

1. Opportunity for control **(AD)**	Discretion, decision latitude, independence, autonomy, job control, self-determination, participation in decision making
2. Opportunity for skill use **(AD)**	Skill utilization and utilization of valued abilities
3. Externally generated goals **(AD)**	Quantitative or qualitative workload, time demands, role responsibility, conflicting demands
4. Variety **(AD)**	Variation in job content and location, non-repetitive work
5. Environmental clarity **(AD)**	Information about the consequences of behaviour (eg availability of feedback), information about the future (eg absence of job future ambiguity), information about required behaviour (eg low role ambiguity)
6. Availability of money **(CE)**	Income level, absence of poverty, material resources
7. Physical security **(CE)**	Absence of danger, good working conditions, ergonomically adequate equipment, safe levels of temperature
8. Opportunity for interpersonal contact **(AD)**	Quantity of interaction (eg contact with others, adequate privacy), quality of interaction (eg good relationship with others, social support)
9. Valued social position **(CE)**	Cultural evaluation of status (eg social rank, occupational prestige), more localized social evaluations of in-company status or job importance
10. Supportive supervision **(AD)**	The extent to which an employee's concerns are taken into account
11. Career outlook **(AD)**	Job security, or the opportunity to gain promotion and to shift to other roles
12. Equity **(CE)**	Justice both within the organization and in relation to wider society.

SOURCE: adapted from Warr (1986) and Warr and Clapperton (2009)

So what?

Those job characteristics which have what Warr calls 'constant effects' have a linear relationship between them and a person's sense of well-being. This continues up to the point at which no further benefit is felt. These are the Vitamin C and E items. A curvilinear relationship or 'additional decrement' is meant to exist between the Vitamin A and D job characteristics and well-being where a moderate level is sufficient but too much or too little will result in negative health effects. Affective, or experienced, well-being is expressed in the model along three dimensions of discontent–content, anxious–comfortable and depressed–pleased. Individuals will react to job characteristics in different ways so it is difficult to predict what definitely will happen. The theory offers managers pointers about how different job characteristics may impact the workforce. Warr acknowledges both that different personality types can be attracted to different types of job and the possibility that gender differences may also moderate the impact of certain job characteristics on well-being (Warr, 1994).

The usefulness of the model is the way it separates out key job character-istics and suggests the way leaders can manage their impact on the overall well-being of the workforce.

What else?

Research on the validity of the theory partially supports Warr's concepts. There are curvilinear relationships between some elements and well-being, although the evidence is mixed and inconclusive for the theory as a whole (De Jonge and Schaufeli, 1998; De Jonge et al, 2000; Sonnentag and Frese, 2003). The general conclusion is that the theory has yet to be fully and empirically investigated (van Veldhoven et al, 2005).

It is worth noting that there is a range of other models and theories related to workplace stress that also consider job characteristics and the wider environment. One of the most well known is the demand-control model developed by Robert Karasek and Törres Theorell (Karasek and Theorell, 1992).

Leadership challenge

What are your present work-based stress levels and how do you think they are affecting your sense of well-being? What can you do to change the situation? How might the lessons about handling stress you have learned from this chapter be used to have a positive impact on the workplace experiences of those you lead?

More help

http://www.hse.gov.uk/

Key reference

Warr, P (1986) A vitamin model of jobs and mental health, in *The Psychology of Work and Organization: Current trends and issues*, ed H W Debus and H W Schroiff, pp 157–64, Elsevier Science, Amsterdam

Other references

Arnold, J and Randall, R (2010) *Work Psychology: Understanding human behaviour in the workplace*, 5th edn, Pearson Education, Harlow

De Jonge, J, Reuvers, M M E N, Houtman, I L D *et al* (2000) Linear and nonlinear relations between psychosocial job characteristics, subjective outcomes, and sickness absence: baseline results from SMASH, *Journal of Occupational Health Psychology*, **5** (2), pp 256–68

De Jonge, J and Schaufeli, W B (1998) Job characteristics and employee well-being: a test of Warr's vitamin model in health care workers using structural equation modelling, *Journal of Organizational Behavior*, **19** (4), pp 387–407

Karasek, R and Theorell, T (1992) *Healthy Work: Stress, productivity, and the reconstruction of working life*, Basic Books, New York

Sonnentag, S and Frese, M (2003) Stress in organizations, in *Comprehensive Handbook of Psychology, vol 12: Industrial and Organizational Psychology*, ed W C Borman, D R Ilgen and R J Klimoski pp. 453–91, Wiley, New York

van Veldhoven, M, Taris, T W, de Jonge, J *et al* (2005) The relationship between work characteristics and employee health and well-being: how much complexity do we really need? *International Journal of Stress Management*, **12** (1), pp 3–28

Warr, P (1994) A conceptual framework for the study of work and mental health, *Work and Stress*, **8** (2), pp 84–97

Warr, P and Clapperton, G (2009) *The Joy of Work? Jobs, happiness, and you*, Taylor & Francis, London

50 What can we do to make our writing more readable?

FOG Index of Readability

The big idea

Robert Gunning, a US college textbook publisher, noticed that many school students seemed unable to understand what they were reading. He took the view that this was due to authors using too many long words and sentences. Writers made it difficult for the reader by creating texts that were full of 'fog'. Gunning spent some years researching readability and in 1944 established the first consultancy specializing in advising other publishers how they could improve their publications. In 1952 he published the first version of a formula that he claimed could measure the readability of any text, the Gunning Fog Index Readability Formula (Gunning, 1952). This has since become known as the FOG Index.

The formula is (Figure 50.1):

1 Select a passage with one or more full paragraphs of around 100 words. Make sure you include all sentences.
2 Calculate the average sentence length by dividing the number of words by the number of sentences.
3 Count the words with three or more syllables. These are the 'complex' words. Don't include proper nouns, familiar jargon or compound words. Also don't include common suffixes (such as -es, -ed or -ing) as a syllable.
4 Add the average sentence length and the percentage of complex words.
5 Multiply the result by 0.4 to give a rating.

(Updated version adapted from Gunning, 1952)

FIGURE 50.1   Calculating the FOG Index

$$0.4\left(\left(\frac{\text{words}}{\text{sentence}}\right) + 100\left(\frac{\text{complex words}}{\text{words}}\right)\right)$$

To make things simpler there are a number of websites that will automatically calculate the FOG Index of a text. These are free and easy to use, giving instant results. Some examples are listed in the More help section below.

A FOG Index of 12 is said to equate to text that will be easily read by university undergraduate students. Anything above is likely to be understood by educated professionals. Text rated at 7 or below will be understood by schoolchildren or people with a similar level of reading ability. Research by Gunning suggests that people tend to buy and read material that is four index levels below the last year they were at school or university. This accounts for the success of newspapers and books that use shorter words and sentence construction.

So what?

Understandable written communication is essential to success in business and professional practice. What people read often determines how they rate a company or an individual. Beyond this, readability, or lack of it, can have serious life consequences. Research on the readability of medical research protocols and patient consent forms has been undertaken using the FOG Index. The findings indicate that for most people such forms are often unreadable (Gazmararian *et al*, 1999; Grossman, Piantadosi and Covahey, 1994). This means that the opportunity for the patient to evaluate risk and medical options for themselves is much reduced.

In a business context, research has found that corporate mission statements are fairly incomprehensible to the average reader (Cochran and David, 1986) and that the publications of successful companies are more readable than those of poorly performing ones (Subramanian, Insley and Blackwell, 1993). For many companies the annual report is a showcase publication that aims to boost investor confidence in the management. However, Courtis and others have found that prose passages in such reports are:

> Beyond the fluent comprehension skills of about 90 per cent of the adult population and about 40 per cent of the investor population. In other words, those responsible for narrative sections of the annual report typically are writing corporate messages at a reading level beyond the educational skills of their target audience.
>
> (Courtis, 1995)

Educators and book authors are also prone to the tendency to overcomplicate written text (Armstrong, 1980; Gillen, 1973). All this points to the importance of training writers to consider the reading skills of their audiences carefully and tailor their work accordingly.

What else?

Readability formulae, of which there are now over 200, have not been immune from criticism. There is an argument that readability is only one aspect of communication. Some subjects, for example, are more difficult than others but understandable because of the expertise of the audience. Presentation style, by the inclusion of graphics and pictures, can help make a text understandable in a way that words alone can't. On the FOG Index specifically, scholars have argued that not all short sentences are easy to read and not all long words are difficult to understand. Similar criticisms have been made of other formulae (Selzer, 1981).

Just for the record, this chapter rates at 9.6 on the FOG Index, apparently making it easily understandable by 14- or 15-year-olds!

Leadership challenge

You are now at model 50. How clear was this book in helping you understand how business psychology can help you? Take one of your recent written reports and test out a sample using one of the free online tests below. What changes do you need to make for your writing to become more understandable to others?

More help

Readability tests online:
http://www.read-able.com/
http://www.online-utility.org/english/readability_test_and_improve.jsp
http://www.readabilityformulas.com/free-readability-formula-assessment.php

Key reference

Gunning, R (1952) *The Technique of Clear Writing*, McGraw-Hill, New York

Other references

Armstrong, J S (1980) Unintelligible management research and academic prestige, *Interfaces*, **10** (2), pp 80–6

Cochran, D S and David, F R (1986) Communication effectiveness of organizational mission statements, *Journal of Applied Communication Research*, **14** (2), pp 108–18

Courtis, J K (1995) Readability of annual reports: Western versus Asian evidence, *Accounting, Auditing and Accountability Journal*, 8 (2), pp 4–17

Gazmararian, J A, Baker, D W, Williams, M V *et al* (1999) Health literacy among Medicare enrollees in a managed care organization, *Journal of the American Medical Association*, **281** (6), pp 545–51

Gillen, B (1973) Readability and human interest scores of thirty-four current introductory psychology texts, *American Psychologist*, **28** (11), pp 1010–11

Grossman, S A, Piantadosi, S and Covahey, C (1994) Are informed consent forms that describe clinical oncology research protocols readable by most patients and their families? *Journal of Clinical Oncology*, **12** (10), pp 2211–15

Selzer, J (1981) Readability is a four-letter word, *Journal of Business Communication*, **18** (4), pp 23–34

Subramanian, R, Insley, R G and Blackwell, R D (1993) Performance and readability: a comparison of annual reports of profitable and unprofitable corporations, *Journal of Business Communication*, **30** (1), pp 49–61